DULAT ISSABEKOV

THE CONFRONTATION

London 2023

Published by Hertfordshire Press Ltd © 2023
e-mail: publisher@hertfordshirepress.com
www.hertfordshirepress.com

THE CONFRONTATION

Play by DULAT ISSABEKOV

collection

English

Translated from Russian by Jonathan Campion,
Timur Akhmedjanov
Edited by Jonathan Campion, Gareth Stamp,
Typeset Alexandra Rey

British Library Catalogue in Publication Data
A catalogue record for this book is available from the British Library
Library of Congress in Publication Data
A catalogue record for this book has been requested

ISBN: 978-1-913356-63-7

CONTENTS

A MAN FROM THE OTHER WORLD

DULAT ISSABEKOV

That was what literary critics and his contemporaries called Dulat Issabekov, when he became a well-known writer of Kazakhstan. When he was just over a year old, Dulat fell seriously ill, and died – or so they thought. The child's body was put out into a cold corridor prior to its burial the following day. Everything was ready for the funeral – the long shirt the child was to be buried in and the meal for the wake after the burial. Then all of a sudden an old lady neighbour, who had been entrusted with the task of handing the infant's body to the grave-diggers, let out a frantic scream. It turned out that the child was still alive, and not just alive, but laughing, after catching sight of the old woman. This was how Dulat returned from the other world just an hour before his funeral was due to start. This happened in 1943, exactly a year after his father had been killed at the Battle of Stalingrad. The writer was to recall: "We were children then, but robbed of our childhood. Our fathers had been lost at the front and our childhood in villages far away from it". Dulat's mother died on the very day he joined the Communist

Youth League aged 14. After that his elder brothers and sisters assumed responsibility for him and he went to a boarding school for orphans in the town of Arys. After leaving school, Dulat became an apprentice fitter in railway communications. In 1961 he gained a place in the philology faculty of the Kazakh State University, from which he graduated in 1966. When Dulat was a student in his final year, a collection of his stories and novellas, entitled "Beket", was published. It was to prove a sensation at the time. The response from critics and readers was a rapturous one. Since 1996 - Member of Kazakhstan Social Democratic Party "Aul". 1966 -1967 - the editor of the Kazakh Radio, served in the Soviet Army. 1971 – Head of "Zhuldyz" Journal ; 1973 - Head of the editorial publishing "Zhalyn"; 1983 - Editor-repertoire of the editorial board of the Ministry of Culture of the Kazakh SSR; 1989 - chief editor of political books; 1991 - General Director of Radio and Television of the Kazakh SSR television. 1992 - Director of the publishing house "Zhazushy." 1998 - Director of the Kazakh Research Institute of Culture and Art. Dulat has always actively engaged in social activities.

He is a member of Arts Council of Kazakhfilm, a member of the political council of the party "Aul", a member of the executive committee of the Kazakh PEN Club. The first story by Dulat Issabekov "The Way" was included in a collection of stories of writers of Kazakhstan called "Contemporary" in 1963, when he was still at university.

In the same year, the most popular newspaper of the time, "Leninshil zhas" published his story "Shoyynkulak" and one day, as they say, he woke up a famous young writer. Literary critics unanimously celebrated his success and unique talent. His stories "Beket", "Gauhar tas", "Notes from a lodger", "Restless Days", "Line of Communication", "Wormwood", "On the sidelines", "Silent", "You did not know war," "Transit passenger" and dozens of others were published one after the other in the press and as a separate book. And in 1980 came the publication of his novel "Kargyn" ("Confusion"), which to this day is very popular, especially among young people. His works "Father's house", "New home in the old house" and "Transit passenger" were published in book form by the Moscow publishing house "Soviet Writer". The novel "Kargyn" "Atamura" (2012); Collection (in 7 volumes). "Atamura", 2012; "Gauhar tas", "Atamura", 2012; Collection of translated works, "Audarma" 2012. Movies of D.Issabekov: "Gauhar tas "(1975); "Wormwood" (1994); "Destiny" (based on the story "Tirshilik", 1998); "Munlyk-Zarlyk" animated film, the studio ("Zhebe") (2010); "Bird of Happiness" - the agency "Khabar" (2011); "The Lottery" - Film studio "Kazakhfilm" S.Aymanov (2012); "The old sister" - TV series. Today Dulat Issabekov has dozens of novellas to his name, around forty short stories and a novel entitled "The Revolt". He has also written over twenty works for the stage. Issabekov's works have been published and republished in Moscow on several occasions. Some of his novellas and stories have been translated into German, Hungarian, Czech and Chinese. Plays by this writer are performed in theatres throughout Kazakhstan. They have also been staged in Turkey, St Petersburg, Omsk, Sofia (Bulgaria), Tajikistan and Bashkortostan. In 2012 a whole international festival was devoted exclusively to his work under the title "The World of Issabekov". Since 2014 his play "The Transit Passenger" has became known in the UK.

Dulat Issabekov was the first writer to be awarded the State Prize of Independent Kazakhstan, the prize of Kazakhstan's PEN Club and the Platinum Prize of the independent organization "Tarlan". Feature films have been made of Issabekov's works "Gaukhar Tas", "Sagebrush", "Far and Away", "Lottery", "Baluan sholak", and also a documentary about his life and work entitled "The World of Issabekov" (2012). In 2014 he received the International Chingiz Aitmatov Award in the House of Lords, British Parliament for his achievements in Literature.

HONOURS: Winner of the M. Auezov Writers' Union (1985, for the play "Muragerler" (Heirs)); Awarded the Order of "Kurmet" (2002); 2009 - the play "Munlyk-Zarlyk" was awarded a grant from the Ministry of Culture and Information; 2010 - the play "Zhauzhyrek" won the Grand Prix in the competition "Tauelsizdik tolgauy"; 2008 - the play "Endi қayttik? .." (What shall we do ?) has been awarded a grant from the Ministry of Culture and Information; Awarded the Order of "Astana" (2008);

Awarded the medal of "Leo Tolstoy", Russia (2012); 2012 - D. Issabekov was awarded the Diploma of the National Academy of Science. Awarded the Order of "Barys" (2012); 2012 - President of Kazakhstan Nursultan Nazarbayev congratulated Dulat Issabekov by special letter.

Dulat Issabekov teaches film courses at the T. Zhurgenov Academy of Arts. He also edits the magazine "Madeniet."

HOUSEWARMING IN AN OLD HOUSE

At the very moment that Yesirkep finished his dinner, the chair beneath him bounced up and down so hard that he nearly fell on the floor. Thinking that it was the antics of his five-year-old son, it did not take long for Yesirkep to slap him on the back. The boy, who at that moment was daydreaming of a Sunday trip to the town's toy shop, began to cry.

'Have you lost your mind?' Yesirkep's wife confronted him.

He started to explain what had happened, but at that moment the chair he was sitting on started to move again. Yesirkep looked at his wife, at his son, and then looked up... The light bulb hanging from the ceiling on a piece of wire was swinging like a pendulum.

'*Oibai!* Everybody outside!' shouted Yesirkep and dashed out of the house. Stopping only in the centre of the yard, he took a breath and looked behind him.

Wife and son were still in the house. '*Oibai!* Kamasiya! Over here! Hurry!' Yesirkep shouted with renewed vigour.

The ground stirred again. Yesirkep, who did not often think of Allah, now called upon him a thousand times for help, then, exhausted with terror, sank to the dust where he stood.

At last his wife appeared in the open doorway. She held their son in her arms.

'Well, did the soul not fly away?' she inquired as she lowered the child from her arms onto the porch.

Yesirkep gradually came to his senses. Seeing that he had unnecessarily hit the child, had rushed out of the house when he should have been thinking of his family, and that he was now sitting in the middle of the yard, Yesirkep felt shame run up and down his body in prickly goosebumps.

'Why are you sitting in the dust like a chicken? Get up!' his wife shouted, nailing him to the ground. 'Look how he treasures his life! And he boasted that as a child he had fought two wolves,' she laughed. 'Don't they have anything better to do than mess with you?'

'Alright, alright,' mumbled Yesirkep, kicking the dust out of his trousers.

'Hurry up and get up! God forbid people should see. You'd better go to your car!

Yesirkep looked around. Thank Allah, there was no one... He tapped his hand once more on his behind, causing a dusty cloud to form there, and went silently out of the gate.

Akzhar used to be considered a large collective farm, but when the consolidation of farms began, the three collective farms were merged into one state farm and Akzhar became just a branch of it. As for Yesirkep, he was transferred from the new central farmstead here to the department as an engine mechanic.

The department had innumerable farms, a shop, bathhouses, a clubhouse, a communications centre.... All this had to be supplied with electricity, but the department was far away from the high-voltage line, and on the orders of the district authorities two electric diesel engines were installed in Akzhar. This made such an impression on the villagers that it was as if a branch of the Moscow metro had passed through their village. Since then every mechanic in the department had dreamed of owning one of the diesels. In pursuit of this cherished goal, the men of Akzhar quietly invited the head of the department, Toiboldy, to a *dastarkhan,* where they initiated him into their dream.

The diesel engines that had been installed raised Toiboldy's profile considerably, elevating him in the eyes of the people of the village. Rumours kept circulating among the villagers that someone would be appointed as a mechanic and others would be rejected by the bosses. One day the director of the state farm called Toiboldy and said that all his candidates were unsuitable, and that Yesirkep could do the diesel work better than anyone else. Two days later Yesirkep's family loaded their belongings onto two tractor carts and moved to Akzhar.

The appointment of an outsider quickly affected the appearance of the ward. Pillars were erected in the winding streets, and real power lines stretched from house to house. Soon a light bulb was flashing outside the office as well. From the first day four subordinates - two assistants and two fitters - were assigned to Yesirkep. Thus, unexpectedly, he became head of the power station and therefore one of the most influential people in Akzhar. Not only that, the director of the state farm made it a habit to take Yesirkep everywhere he went, which was a great blow to Toiboldy, and in time became the main reason for his increased pressure.

That year, the villagers in the ward were buying television sets by the dozen from the shop, and after a month of this competition, an aerial appeared above every house. The ever-proud parents, Ombai and Dombai, who would talk everywhere about their modest means, were among the first to buy colour televisions.

Yesirkep was beginning to come into his own. He no longer agreed to everyone's invitations to visit, and if he did go to a *dastarkhan*, it was only for a short time, as befits a respectable, busy leader. But then the youngest daughter of the head of MTM suddenly married the eldest son of the current director, and Yesirkep had to participate in the celebration. Hearing a respectful '*Es-aga*' from all sides, Yesirkep suddenly reported loudly:

'I fought two wolves as a child and skinned them both…'

It went very quiet.

'You must have had a gun,' someone suggested politely. But at these words Yesirkep started up like a diesel.

'What rubbish! I was unarmed. These hands and nothing else!' Yesirkep showed the villagers his hands.

'I don't believe you,' said a daring young man, thoroughly warmed up by the feast. 'How could you, when even Tashkenbai sitting in front of you was armed to the teeth, but he still ran without a backward glance from a single wolf…'

Yesirkep exploded.

'What's that got to do with anything? He is Tashkenbai and I am Yesirkep!' he shouted, trying to remember whether or not the man's house had paid for its electricity. An argument broke out. The feast was divided into two camps, some taking the lad's side, some of them with Yesirkep.

'Let's go and see which of you is tougher!' the young man teased. 'When you were a child you skinned two wolves. And Tashkenbai ran away from one. Now let's go and see who's braver now. Tasheke, are you ready?'

'I'm ready!' Tashkenbai shouted fiercely. His mood did not please Yesirkep, but realising that he could no longer be silent, he declared that he was as ready as he had ever been.

The wife knew her husband. Fearing that Yesirkep was likely to embarrass himself, she chose a moment to whisper to him:

'Come on now… It's embarrassing in front of the principal…'

'Why should I stop?' raged Yesirkep. 'Even if Allah himself is present, Yesirkep knows the value of his honour. Hey, who wants to come out? Let's go!'

The fight would take place at the mare's stall under the canopy. The lights had not yet been switched on. The young man who made the commotion switched on the headlights of the Zhiguli which was parked at the mare's stall. Old men and old women, girls and young women, boys and girls, the whole staff of the department were watching the fight with interest. The head of the department, Toiboldy, tried to prevent the fight, but it did not work - the sides were relentless. Knowing that the principal was sympathetic to Yesirkep, and bearing in mind his imminent retirement, Toiboldy lost his head in despair.

The fight ended as quickly as it had begun. Yesirkep moved menacingly towards his opponent, but the latter suddenly used an unknown technique, and Yesirkep was soon seeing all the stars in the sky. The one who had once fled from a wolf did not stop there: he twisted the arms of his lying adversary and sat down on him. Then he took some cigarettes out of his pocket and smoked nonchalantly.

Unable to stay in the crowd, Kamasiya grabbed the child and went back to the house. The department head Toiboldy, knowing there would be a big scandal, also slipped out of the crowd and escaped into the darkness as a precaution.

Yesirkep climbed out from under the winner, looked intently at the fans and walked towards the power station. He burst into the duty officer's cabinet like an enraged bull. Shiftman Zhumat was dozing, resting his forehead on an oily metal table. When he saw the boss appear before him Zhumat shouted in a hysterical voice:

‘No! I wasn’t asleep!’

‘Turn it off!’ commanded Yesirkep.

‘No, I wasn’t sleeping! I never sleep on the job!’ cried Zhumat.

‘What are you jabbering about? Turn it off. Turn the engine off!

‘Why?

‘Do it!’

‘Yes... How come...? People... They’ll file a complaint...’

‘Let them. Say the alternator’s burnt out, the cylinder’s jammed. Just shut it down!

After a minute the roar of the diesel engine ceased and the village was plunged into pitch darkness. He climbed up onto the roof of the hut, looked in the direction of the house where the celebration was taking place, listened with satisfaction to the babble of the bewildered people, and said to his subordinate:

‘If anyone asks, you haven’t seen me.’

At home, Yesirkep cursed angrily and collapsed onto the bed.

‘Hey, you’ll frighten the children, go into the other room,’ Kamasiya interrupted him. ‘A man should know his limits. Shame on the whole village... And now your engine’s stalled.’

At night Yesirkep snored as if he was being strangled. Convinced that it was impossible to sleep next to him, his wife moved the children into the next room and shut the doors tightly.

Toiboldy came around at dawn. We have to fix the station by all means, he said. He was followed by the MTM superintendent. One by one the head of the club, the watchmen of the bathhouse, shops and warehouses came in. They all heard the same reply: 'The diesel is out of order. Until a spare part is delivered from the centre, there will be no power'.

In the afternoon the street in front of Yesirkep's house turned into a bazaar. In the evening the second episode of Kyz-Zhibek was to be shown, and the people of Akzhar were begging and pleading with Yesirkep. All of his ancestors (up to the seventh generation), he and his offspring were praised so much that it seems even Allah could not resist. Yesirkep did not lift a finger. He himself, when he lived on the central farmstead, had already watched the film, so he couldn't have been calmer.

'You've got golden hands! You can do anything...'

'What do you mean, a jammed cylinder? For a master like you that's a piece of cake,' came the familiar voice of a young man, feeling the insults of the day before gradually fading away.

'We gave that rascal a good reprimand,' someone

in the crowd said, unaware that he was tapping at the power station manager's sore spot. 'He doesn't know how to escape shame; he says he may forgive me, and I am ready to present him with a horse and a *chapan*! He slaughtered a sheep and is humbly waiting for you in his house. Please, do your best, and give us some light for the evening.

'To fix the cylinder is...' Yesirkep began very weightily, about to give his consent.

But then someone in the crowd said:

'If you trust me, the MTM mechanics will fix it,' he announced, screwing up the whole thing.

Yesirkep faltered again. But the young man immediately shut the impatient one up:

'Are there any worthwhile young men in the MTM?! Nobody here is capable of fixing the cylinder. Stay there and shut up,' he shouted.

'Okay,' said Yesirkep, with a sigh. 'If that's what people want, I'll try. There will be light in the evening!

'Hurrah! What a guy! That's the boy!' people began to disperse slowly.

When he arrived at the power station, he took apart the innocent generator and the intact motor for show. While he had promised to have light by the evening, Yesirkep was at a loss when he saw the pile of parts. When the roar of the diesel engine sounded in the twilight, Yesirkep was overjoyed. Coming up to the panel, Yesirkep switched on the switch. The electric lights above the village shone.

Knowing that they were coming for him, he hurried home as soon as the engine started.

Taking his wife with him, he got into the car that had been sent for him. Just as importantly he stepped into the courtyard of his victor. He answered the people's greetings with importance. He took food from the *dastarkhan*. Before Kyz-Zhibek started the *kuirdak* had been eaten. For some reason the master of the house did not show his face. Every now and then Yesirkep glanced towards the door, waiting for the moment when he would come and ask for forgiveness. But that moment did not come.

It was about ten minutes before the film started. When all the guests had settled in front of the television screen and were clamouring for silence, there was a sudden shout from the street. Yesirkep recognised the voice; it was Tashkenbai.

'Oooh, you wretches! Pay, pay for my sheep! You'll pay me for it, you freeloaders!' heard Yesirkep and felt that something unforeseen had happened.

Tashkenbai showed up ten minutes before the film started. He was wet and dirty. Unspeakably surprised by the unexpected feast in his own house, he asked why there was a celebration, but it was difficult to understand the people's reason, and Tashkenbai started shouting:

'Get out! I'll kill them all! Where's that blabbermouth? I'll show him how to turn out the lights when there's a wedding.'

The people all jumped on Tashkenbai in droves.

'*Oibai*, my brothers, calm your anger. We're all doing this as friends. Why are you jumping on Yesirkep? Yesterday you smoked while sitting on him, isn't that enough? Tomorrow you'll get two sheep from us. We only wanted your name. So you won't suffer a loss. Better go and say hello to Yesirkep. Kyz-Zhibek is starting in three minutes.' People were pressing on all sides, and Tashkenbai had to give in.

When the film started, he, supported on both sides, was already sitting by the television, occasionally dropping his head on his chest. Astonished at what was happening on the screen, Tashkenbai shouted out, 'Oh, God!' He glared fiercely at Yesirkep, but allowed himself nothing more.

However, this incident undermined Yesirkep's hitherto unquestionable authority. *Uzun-Kulak* had done his dirty work, and even on the central homestead there were some snide jokes about Yesirkep, so that he now had an excuse for stopping the station every day.

Gradually he resumed his humility and silently endured the taunts.

Today he was quite sure that no one had noticed his behaviour during the earthquake, but for some reason the rumour spread throughout the village. In the evening he came home angry and attacked his wife from the doorstep:

'I will kick you out! Divorce! If it comes to that, Yesirkep can do without his wife. Go back to your parents!'

His wife knew what had happened.

'What's got into you?' she asked calmly, putting the noodles into the pan. 'Have you slept with evil spirits?'

'Urgh, wretch,' cried Yesirkep. 'The rumour has spread all over the village, and now she pretends not to understand anything. Who but you saw me hit the child?'

'Stop talking nonsense!' said Kamasiya as she continued with her noodles. 'Change your clothes, wash your hands and sit down at the table. Dinner is ready.'

'Don't change the subject! Who else could have told those chatterboxes how I hit the child and jumped out of the house?'

'Who could have told? Your son did. He's been playing outside all day.'

Yesirkep, bewildered by this simple explanation, was momentarily confused.

Kamasiya hummed into her palm and, unable to restrain herself, clutched her stomach and laughed until she cried. Yesirkep became alarmed.

'Hey, hey, that's enough! The children will hear you!' he hissed miserably in a voice that had settled with confusion. And then he ran out into the street.

If a Kazakh starts to make a fuss over someone, no good can come of it. Yesirkep's peers were tirelessly spreading new stories about him, presenting fiction as truth, and turning the truth into God's punishment. Who would have thought that people had such a good memory!

Lately there had been talk in the village that the department would be connected to a high-voltage line and there would be no need for a power station. Some preparatory work had even been carried out...

It was the first year that Yesirkep got a holiday. He spent it on the Black Sea coast. His friends saw him off noisily. While Yesirkep was resting, the department was connected to the AEP...

Yesirkep was welcomed by all his peers who lived in Akzhar. In the railway station restaurant they celebrated the return of their comrade. Tarakbai, having softened up, complained to Yesirkep, who was unspeakably pleased with the welcome he had received.

'After you left, that backstabber got cocky.'

'Yes, there's something to be said about him,' Tashkenbai seconded, nodding his elongated head.

'What happened?' Yesirkep looked around at them all and asked. 'What's he all worked up about?'

'Alright, tell him everything!' said Tarakbai with bitter determination. 'Remember when his eldest son married the youngest daughter of the MTM superintendent, there was a misunderstanding between them?'

'Well...' Yesirkep tensed up.

'So, now the youngest daughter of the station manager is getting married to the eldest son of the MTM manager. Tonight is their wedding night. Zavtokom says he will never forget Yesirkep's shenanigans, neither in this world nor in the next. It is better for him if he stays as far away from our party as possible. We told him that you were not to blame for this, but the old man said that if you spoil the feast a second time, he will tie your hands and send you to the place where they ride dogs. He didn't invite your wife to the wedding either. We all fought over it at the back of the house and said that if your family was not invited to the wedding, we would not go either.'

'Thank you,' said Yesirkep excitedly. 'So you weren't invited...'

'It's a good thing you're here tonight, to spite him by turning off the engine and going to bed. Don't go outside. If he really comes at you, we won't stay away.'

Yesirkep was anxious to get to the village as quickly as possible. His friends had been stoking his resentment and anger all the way...

The car stopped in front of the station. As soon as Yesirkep opened the door, Zhumat jumped out of the office, as if on cue, and smiled at the boss apologetically.

'Shut it off!' commanded Yesirkep.

'What?

'The engine.'

'How did we break down? Is the cylinder jammed?

'Say it's broken, that's all!'

'Will do.'

The people standing in the back made a ruckus:

'Yeah! Let's go! Zhumat will shut it down himself as well.

Yesirkep got in the car and slammed the door with a crack.

There was indeed a wedding going on at the house behind the gate. The young man, having dropped Yesirkep off at his house, drove away quickly.

He took the key from the hand-washing stand and entered the house. 'The poor woman,' he decided, 'must be staying with the neighbours; she cannot have fun at the wedding because of me.' He suddenly felt pity for his wife and children. He was deeply moved and lay down to listen to the sounds from the street...

He woke up to loud voices.

'Oh, I think your dad's here! That's right, his suitcase!' He heard his wife's voice and finally woke up.

'Well, where do you go, you little foals!' He got up from the cushions, fumbled with the children in the dark and kissed them.

'Why are you lying in the dark? Shall I turn on the light?' said the wife.

'We'll talk about that later... There will be no light today,' said Yesirkep. 'Light the paraffin lamp.'

'What do you mean "later"?' What happened to the lights? Come on!' His wife flicked the switch, and the bulb on the string under the ceiling flashed dazzlingly.

'Oooh, the dog! Still not jammed!' Yesirkep frowned and began to put on his boots.

'Where are you going? You're crazy!' His wife snapped her hands in a sorrowful voice.

Yesirkep, wasting no time, jumped out into the street. The village was flooded with bright light. Yesirkep listened... The diesels were silent. He staggered on, lost in thought, when suddenly, like lightning, an idea flashed into his mind...

‘Listen, those four were giggling suspiciously when they came to the wedding,’ Kamasiya said thoughtfully. ‘Maybe they are up to something again...?’

‘Who are you talking about?’

The wife said who she was referring to...

Yesirkep stood in one place for a long time. Then, exhausted, he sank down on the block and wept.

At dawn he knocked on the door of the head of the department. Toiboldy was still asleep. When he opened his eyes and saw Yesirkep leaving for the Black Sea, with a face that looked as if he had just killed a man, the head of the department pulled his head away from the pillow.

‘Oh... Wh-what happened?

‘Two carts are needed,’ Yesirkep muttered. ‘What do you need carts for? Is everything alright?!’ ‘Everything is alright. Give me two carts. I’ll bring them back in the evening.’

When he received the carts, Yesirkep began noisily loading his belongings into them.

‘Where the hell are you going?’ cried his wife, followed by the children.

‘Wherever you go... Shut up! Shut up!’ Yesirkep shouted, throwing things at the carts.

When almost all the belongings had been packed,

a crowd of old men, led by Tarakbai, suddenly came into the courtyard of his house. Among them were the four men. Struggling to comprehend after yesterday's feast what was going on in Yesirkep's house, they looked at the tractor carts full of household belongings for a long time... Finally, having understood what was going on, Tashkenbai clutched his head:

'Forgive us, we are such fools! How were we supposed to know you'd be so worried?!' He wailed hysterically.

By lunchtime, the belongings had been unloaded and put back in their places. Tarakbai cut up a sheep and the others ran to the shop.

In the evening, a big toast was held at Yesirkep's house. All four of them repeatedly asked for forgiveness. And they wept tears of remorse. Yesirkep also wiped his eyes with a handkerchief. Tashkenbai raised his glass and made a toast:

'Happy housewarming!

'What bastards you are,' said Yesirkep, smiling happily.

1984

OPERATION STATUE

No sooner had Party Secretary Zhanaidarov entered his office in the early hours of the morning, combed his hair, brushed the traces of dandruff from his shoulders and sat down in a chair, than the telephone rattled loudly in the corner to his right, as if just waiting for him to arrive. 'Long distance,' thought Zhanaidarov, picking up the receiver and holding it to his ear. 'Hello!' he uttered in an important, somewhat tired voice, preoccupied with the enormity of things to do in the morning. 'Zhanaidarov speaking. Ah, hello, Tursun Satanovich!' The trace of importance went from his voice, and he seemed ready to hang up the phone. 'How is your health? I heard you caught a cold, how do you feel now? Is it gone? Yes, spring is the most treacherous time, especially the beginning. You should take care of yourself, dress warmer. I say, take care of yourself. From colds, I mean... Yes? I remember, of course. You bet I do! A statue? Statue! It's... standing... Right in front of the tannery. Who, who? Well...' Zhanaidarov suddenly weakened and became as helpless as a steppe toad seeing a snake: sucked in, hypnotised. 'Let them come... Let them... Wait... You too...?' his voice quivered. '*Oibai*, in that case... Of course we are, we're delighted, infinitely delighted. When, when? This evening...? Where did you say the guests come from? From England...? Oh, thank Allah... Save... ' Zhanaidarov had no time to come to his senses; they had already hung up the phone at the other end.

'That's it, gone!' he whispered as if reciting a last prayer. 'This is God's punishment, pure and simple. Who would have thought it! And these Englishmen get themselves around the world. They should be sitting there on their own island, but they have to go all the way from one side of the world to the other. Not only to England, but to Alma-Ata!'

Zhanaidarov himself did not notice how he rose from his desk and paced around the room, putting his hands behind his back. An unknowable force, blowing out from the telephone receiver, lifted him easily from his chair and made him pace like a pendulum around the study.

Here, perhaps, it is necessary to explain why the district secretary was so agitated.

OPERATION STATUE

The area had long been a livestock breeding area. Even in the pre-revolutionary years, this region was famous for its fat flocks of sheep. That's why a meat processing plant was built here in its time. If it was a meat processing factory, it should also have a leather processing plant. As it was found out later, this workshop was the first one in Kazakhstan, which later grew into the biggest combine in the country. Last year the whole district, region and even the entire republic was eagerly preparing to celebrate the centenary of the combine. During these preparations various meetings were held with the combine's workers. Radio and TV broadcasts were arranged, and artists and writers began visiting the combine. During one of these meetings a guest, a writer from Alma-Ata, came to the podium and said: 'We have forgotten how to appreciate and honour the working man. Who laid the foundation of this factory? Who was the first owner of this workshop? It is necessary to find the first tanner of leather and erect a statue to him in front of the mill! And we must do it quickly!' A storm of applause greeted his words. It lasted for quite a long time. The orators who stood on the podium cheered the writer, who had become a prophet to them. They demanded the speedy erection of such a statue and even issued a public shakedown to the district authorities, for not thinking about it sooner.

So a paper proposing the construction of a statue in honour of the first tanner went to the region, and from the region to the republic, and from there as far away as the centre. Six months passed, and only then did the paper, tired to the point of exhaustion, finally return to the district. There was no sign of the endless resolutions on it, and it was accompanied by accompanying, tongue-in-cheek letters. And this paper, shaking its leaflet tongue like a ribbon of rags in shreds from a dervish's head, was laid on the table in front of Zhanaidarov, tempted and shabby.

In short, the question of erecting the statue was resolved in principle, as they say. Now another question arose: how to depict the first tanner: full-length or only as a bust? Artists, for example, or writers can be placed on statues in different poses; they can stand, or sit, or recline on a plinth, but it seems awkward to truncate the working man's lower part. And so, in the end, it was decided that it had to be full-length.

After that they sent another paper to Alma-Ata with a plea: 'So, so and so, send us a sculptor, and not some run-of-the-mill one, but the very best one.

A week later two men arrived from Alma-Ata. The head of the propaganda and agitation department was pleased to say they would be received.

'Let them in,' Zhanaidarov said, adjusting his tie.

Two men entered the office with eyes as deep as a well in the desert. One's hair was braided into pigtails; the other's completely covered his shoulders. At the sight of them, Zhanaidarov shuddered.

After shaking hands, the two noticed that Zhanaidarov was looking at them incredulously, even squeamishly, and handed over their passports.

'Durus,' said Zhanaidarov, clearly wishing to get rid of them as soon as possible. 'Get on with it.'

'When do you need it?'

Zhanaidarov looked at the head of the department, and asked 'When is it due?'

'By autumn,' said the head of the department. 'By the twenty-fourth of October. That's when the centenary celebrations are scheduled. Will you be able to do it by that date?

'Easy,' said the one with the pigtails.

'A piece of cake!' he chimed in, his hair falling down over his shoulders. Immediately a contract was concluded and signed with the sculptors and an advance was given.

The hardest part started now. What should the statue be like? Is it enough to take the figure of a worker and cast it, or should it be tanned? Should the portrait be a resemblance of someone, or can it be a common type? Or should it be a close relative, a descendant of the first tanner? Maybe someone from the local community? Someone off the street? Somewhere in these parts or from far away? From here? In fact, what was the name of this pioneer in the tanning business? When was he born, when did he die? What was his appearance, his character, his demeanor? And so on and so forth...

While the two sculptors were figuring it all out, two more months passed. The master's direct descendants were also found. It turned out that they live in the area, and one of them even lived near the district committee. They also found out the name of the first leather tanner and prepared an official text to be engraved on the plinth: 'Melden Zheldibayev, the founder of leather tanning in Kazakhstan'. Ashten Zheldibayev, a living descendant of his distant relative, turned out to be a plumber in house management office number two. He described in detail what Melden looked like, sketched his height, face, his whole appearance - all according to the words of his father, who remembered the old tanner well. When his grandson finally produced a portrait of Melden on paper, he bore a close resemblance to the narrator, Ashten. The artists, or sculptors, themselves sat for a long time in astonishment, looking silently at the portrait and back at Ashten.

'So your distant kinsman is your exact copy?' the two beards marvelled.

'Yes, according to those who saw my grandfather, he looked like me, as if he had been skinned and stuffed.'

'I'm sorry, maybe it's you who looks like him, not him who looks like you? After all, he is somewhat older than you…'

'Yes,' laughed the plumber, 'Maybe so.'

In short, they decided to make a sculptural portrait of Melden directly from Ashten. They measured his height, thickness and even the length of his fingers and got down to business. Ashten started coming to the House of Culture every evening after work. He came to the room where the two sculptors had set up their studio. He lifted the hide of a Yolbayev ram high above his head with both hands and stared at it lovingly for hours. And the two artists, who were also sculptors, made sketches of it from both sides.

So some twenty sketches had already been made of Ashten holding the skin over his head. The sculptors had to, on arrival back in Alma-Ata, make a sample statue of the one they liked best, mould it in clay, and then do the same in plaster.

The unknown Ashten, who until then had been quietly drinking his red wine in the cellars of houses, suddenly became one of the most famous people in the village. A number of people were honoured to say hello to the model for the statue of the first tanner, and some were happy to walk down the street to the liquor shop with him and buy him a bottle. Some even took pride in standing in line with him. All this could not help but excite the district leaders. 'As long as the work on the statue is unfinished, keep an eye on Ashten. No matter what happens!' Zhanaidarov himself once expressed his fears, and this was taken as an order. To avoid Ashten putting himself at risk on the town's streets, it was decided that a bottle of pure wheat vodka would be secretly brought to him from the district committee's cupboard, one every two days... So that no one would suspect anything, they began to carry the potion in bottles of Sary-Agach mineral water. But Ashten was Ashten: one time he took his dose of 'mineral water' and then went to a park, where he asked someone's girlfriend to dance. She refused, which led to a scandal, and the scandal ended in a fight, so in the end Ashten had to have a ride in a yellow car with a blue stripe. When at the police station the police lieutenant began to fill in a form for Ashten's fifteen-day arrest, Ashten squeezed his hand tightly and asked

'Can I call the district?'

The lieutenant smirked:

'Don't you want to call the UN? Go ahead. Perez de Cuellar is in Cebu's office right now.

'I... I am... telling the truth...' Ashten almost fell out of his chair, but managed to grab hold of the edge of the table.

The senior lieutenant and the lieutenant looked at each other. 'Shall I let him make a call?' asked the lieutenant. 'Let's see what he has to say. We can have a laugh!'

He smiled and nodded.

Ashten, wobbling on his feet, not without difficulty dialed four numbers, then coughed.

The two policemen smiled merrily, enjoying the fun.

Finally a bass voice came through the receiver:

'The district committee's duty officer speaking,' he said clearly in the silence.

'Hello... Duty officer... It's me... Ashten,' said the detainee. He was stammering, though he tried not to.

'Who?

'Ashten, Zheldybayev... Ashten... Statue... You know, the one they're making the statue from... I'm the one... They want to put me in jail... Where? For fifteen days... Yes!' Ashten turned to the lieutenants. They sat relaxed, smiling, not quite sure what was happening.

'Address... What is your address?' Ashten asked.

They exchanged a glance.

District police station. Every idiot knows this.

Ashten smacked his swollen lips against the tube again.

The district police station... They say every idiot knows...

Ashten hung up the phone and sat back in his chair.

Not ten minutes later he was picked up by the car on duty.

The two policemen remained seated, unsure whether this had happened in a dream or in reality.

The case raised Ashten's profile even higher.

Time went by, and eventually the sculptors from Alma-Ata said that they couldn't make it by the deadline, i.e. the twenty-fourth of October. The district wrote to the region to have the centenary celebrations timed to coincide with the November holidays.

But even by 7 November the statue was not ready. A letter was again sent to the region, arguing that the best time to celebrate the anniversary of the tannery was on New Year's Eve.

But the statue was not ready for the new year either. Then the region, as they say, became enraged. The district was accused of failing to keep its word, and the issue of neglected cultural work on the part of district leaders was considered at a meeting, at which Zhanaidarov tried to justify himself and, it must be said, not in the best way. 'The statue is almost ready,' he lied without looking at anyone. 'Only minor details remain: the nose, for example, the eyes and the ears, or rather one ear. This softened the blow and warded off more serious punishments. 'Well, if it's only the nose, two eyes and one ear, then never mind,' the region consoled. 'And yet, when exactly will the statue be ready?' they asked menacingly. 'Does the whole figure have to suffer because of such trifles as eyes, noses and everything else? Will it take five days to glue it all on?'

But even after five days the statue was not ready. He was still noseless, eyeless and earless, but the district could not, so to speak, lose face, and reported back to the region: 'The statue is ready'.

The news that a statue honouring the first tanner in Kazakhstan was to be erected quickly spread around the county. This was widely reported in the district, regional and national press, and even in the central newspaper, Pravda. It seems that the news reached abroad from there. The result was that a delegation from far-away England had the misfortune of visiting the Paradise Centre where it would be unveiled.

And yet the statue was still not ready. What to do...?

'Well, what shall we do?' Zhanaidarov asked,

gathering his senior staff members in his office. 'Representatives of the tannery from England, accompanied by the secretary of the Regional Committee, are coming to visit us tonight. In the morning they want to see the factory, and of course, they want to admire the statue of the first tanner. What can we do, how can we get out of this?

No one opened their mouth.

'What if we say someone knocked down the statue in the night?' suggested the head of the agriculture department.

'No way,' objected the head of the department. 'And if they say to find the criminals, who should we grab by the neck? It is better to tell the truth and admit our guilt. Perhaps he himself, Comrade Secretary, will find a convenient excuse to take away from us... foreigners.'

Zhanaidarov glared at him angrily:

'Then we're all dead. There's no patronage for cheating at the Obkom.'

'What to do?'

'What to do?'

No one could suggest anything sensible.

'And it's raining at the wrong time,' the head of the livestock department broke the silence again by talking about the weather.

'What's the rain got to do with it?' The chief of propaganda scowled at him, unhappy with the inappropriate conversation his neighbour had started.

There was again a pained silence.

'I didn't start this conversation for nothing,' the head of the agriculture department went on. 'Even though we reported on the statue, it hasn't been officially unveiled yet. By the time the British delegation and guests from the region arrive, the wooden pillar which is sticking out on the plinth must be removed, and Ashten himself must be put in its place - temporarily, of course. The unveiling of the statue will take, I think, no more than ten minutes; well, a fortnight at most. We'll hurry them up ourselves. Ashten can drink free 'Sary-Agach' for six months if he agrees to stand motionless for half an hour with a lamb's skin in his outstretched hands. Nothing will happen to Ashten, although it is raining. When the delegation leaves, he will jump off the plinth and go home.'

'What's half an hour?' laughed the head of the general department out loud. 'Let him stand during the day and go home to sleep in the evening. We'll find another plumber to replace him at night.'

The people, who had been sitting silently as if at a funeral, laughed loudly and amicably.

'Comrades, stop laughing!' exclaimed Zhanaidarov angrily. 'This is no time for jokes. Who has any other suggestions?'

'There's no point in wasting your time. We have to accept the idea,' said the head of the livestock department himself.

Zhanaidarov grabbed his head with his hand and paced vigorously around the room in front of the assembled subordinates, who were tensely silent, like children seeing a school and a teacher for the first time.

'I think we have to accept this idea too,' said the head of the office firmly, 'We have no other option.'

It was as if the cabinet exploded! There were questions everywhere as to whether Ashten should be placed on a plinth or not, and if he was, what if he sneezed or coughed in the presence of foreign guests and the Secretary of the Communist Party?

The district leader had to think long and hard.

In the end, the question was put to a vote.

The bureau unanimously decided that the plumber Ashten Zheldybayev should stand for one hour on the plinth in front of the tannery building. The guests were arriving that evening and would inspect the statue in the morning. Therefore, a group of three or four people must work with Ashten in advance, persuade and caress him to stand on the plinth for an hour, while trying not to anger him, not to step on any sore points, and speak with the utmost care and subtlety, as if they were pulling a horse's hair out of a ball of dough.

A group of district committee instructors arrived at Ashten's house. Ashten, reclining on the sofa in front of the television set, opened the door to them because they said they were 'from the district committee'. The men surrounded Ashten, prodded him, persuaded him, intimidated him, and promised him almost the moon. In the end they persuaded him to agree to stand for an hour as a living statue on a plinth. When he gave a muffled 'alright,' it was as if a mountain had been lifted from their shoulders. They wiped the sweat from their foreheads with a sigh of relief.

'But be warned, I will not stand still for a minute after the time is up. I don't give a damn about your Englishmen, I'll jump off and go home,' was Ashten's way of expressing his stubborn nature.

'Look out, the secretary of the Communist Party will be there too.'

'So what? He's something for you, but he's nothing to me. And what kind of a secretary is he if he couldn't get a single statue built in all this time! Who needs a secretary like that?' Ashten delivered a long tirade that struck fear and terror into the hearts of the instructors.

After patting Ashten on the back, almost licking him, the men from the district committee left.

Three cars arrived on the promised date and the distinguished foreign guests arrived. They were received with proper fanfare, accommodated in a special hotel, and served a fancy dinner... Both our and their leaders took the floor: the leader of the British delegation expressed admiration for the inventiveness of the Soviet people and their leaders, who had erected the first statue of a simple leather tanner, their great and tender love of history, their special attention and care for a simple working man, their love of art and refined artistic taste, and raised a toast to their health. Our side did not lose face either. The secretary of the regional committee in his speech noted that the statue erected here in honour of the unknown worker is a kind of sign that such a thing is possible only in a socialist society, and there is no such thing in capitalistic society; that he is extremely glad and proud that such a statue had been erected not just anywhere, but exactly in that part of the world where they were standing now; that statues can take the form of a bust or also show the lower part of a person. At this the English party applauded in unison and the representatives of the district committee looked at each other. He went on to inform the English guests that tomorrow’s programme would be too full and tight in terms of schedule, so the viewing had to take place today and would happen immediately after dinner. The English party began to argue that the viewing had been scheduled for the next morning, after breakfast, and that viewing the statue in the evening was, to put it mildly, a sign of 'bad manners', to which the district manager replied that it is a forced measure, otherwise they would not have time to visit the village seventy kilometres away, where the shepherds would serve them hot kebabs made of freshly skinned mutton in the open air. Wouldn't that be preferable to gazing all morning at the figure of a tanner with a sheep skin in his outstretched hands? Each member of the delegation was to be given photographs of the statue, taken from different angles. The foreigners clapped their hands together again, signifying their acceptance of the changed programme.

While the guests were eating dinner, a group of men from the district committee again turned up at Ashten's place and with all sorts of apologies. They began to explain to him that the programme had suddenly changed and he would have to go up on the plinth tonight instead of in the morning.

'Alright,' he said, stretching out his hand to the trousers hanging from the headboard. 'I'll stand up for the district committee!'

'But not a word about this to anyone! Even your wife must not know about it.'

'Why?

One of the young men hurriedly took out an envelope and handed it to Ashten. He opened the envelope, peered into it, and silently slipped it into his trouser pocket.

'Three,' said the young man who had passed the envelope, 'then you'll get two more.'

'Isn't that a bit small?

'Have a conscience!' One of the instructors burst into tears. 'Five hundred roubles for half an hour! That's your salary for four months.'

Ashten, who had already put one foot in his trouser leg, began to pull it back out.

The young man who handed over the envelope grabbed Ashten's trouser leg.

'My dear man, don't take your trousers off, I beg you! It was just a thought. It just came out of his mouth. Didn't it, eh?' He turned to his companion, winked, and told him off.

'I didn't mean to,' he apologised slyly. 'I wonder how it came out of my mouth…'

Ashten began to pull on the other trouser leg. Finally, having dressed Ashten up like a bride for a dress fitting, they picked him up from under his arms, led him out the door, and only then did he breathe a sigh of relief.

'Where are you taking him in the middle of the night?' his wife shouted after them.

Ashten turned around and proudly said: 'Stay out of the district committee's business!'

***

When the British approached the square in front of the combine, Ashten was already standing on the plinth, staring at the dried lambskin that he held high in his outstretched hands. The lights, all of them directed onto the statue, made the statue look huge and majestic. Zhanaidarov himself was struck by this view of the statue.

The English guests walked around the statue, respectfully and admiringly looking at it with the most enthusiastic words. 'Amazing!', 'wonderful!' 'Rare art!' came to Zhanaidarov's ears, and with each passing moment he felt more and more excited, his heart clenched tightly as if fine needles were being thrust into it.

Don't let them be too long, take them away quickly,' he whispered to the instructor as he walked past and looked at the Communist Party secretary for ideology with great respect.

Averting his eyes, he raised his face to the sky and sighed. Then he noticed a trickle of white steam escaping from his mouth. It was only now that he remembered that the rain that had fallen in the morning and towards the end of the day had turned to snow, and he saw flakes of snow that whipped around the sharp beams of the searchlight, and the white, slightly thawed, shoulder straps of Ashten's black overcoat. He stood motionless, bravely exposing his face to the falling snow, and Zhanaidarov admired the selflessness of the plumber. He even felt pity for him in his heart.

Despite the fact that the secretary of the district party committee hurried things along, the foreign guests kept walking around the statue, and were in no rush to leave the square in front of the factory. They wanted to know where the stone for the plinth had come from, when it was erected, who first came up with the idea of commemorating the first master of leather tanning, who the sculptor was, and what school and style was favoured. In general, they completely messed with Zhanaidarov's head. He barely had time to fend off the questions that were falling like snow from the dark sky. At one point he noticed with horror that the secretary of the regional committee for ideology had come up to them and was also listening in silence. 'Praise to Allah!' he thought, frightened by his lies about the stone being transported from afar and other details about the statue. 'How badly it must have turned out for me. And the devil dared me to get involved with that statue!'

'It's a pity! A pity!' 'The lanky Englishman was wiping the lens of his camera with his handkerchief.

'What is he talking about?' Zhanaidarov asked the interpreter anxiously.

'He regrets not visiting the statue during the day,' he explained.

'You explain to them that there will be another dastarkhan. And being late for a dastarkhan is considered shameful in our society. Tell them,' the ideological secretary demanded of the interpreter.

'Oh! Tastarkhan!' cried the long-haired Englishman. 'Opyat tastarkhan!'

'Da, da, da,' said the secretary of the Communist Party, calling everyone to his side with a broad gesture. 'The Kazakhs like to eat meat late at night!'

The interpreter immediately translated the words.

'Uh-oh! Shkotland!' another Brit exclaimed. 'I'm a Scotsman. We like our scran too...' The last words were said in English, and when the interpreter translated them into Kazakh everyone laughed in unison.

The secretary of the regional committee said a warm goodbye to everyone and left for the regional centre. Before leaving, he took Zhanaidarov aside: 'Your statue is a success. It is standing here as if it were alive. It's a very realistic statue,' he praised. 'It should be nominated for the State Prize!'

'Oh dear, oh dear!' muttered Zhanaidarov, completely losing his head at these words.

'What's the matter with you? You are shivering so much, are you ill or something?'

'No, no! I'm... touched by your words!'

No sooner had the black Volga disappeared from view than someone's soul-shattering shriek was heard by the plinth. Everyone involuntarily looked around. The long-haired Englishman, who was about to take a picture of the statue, froze with his head up and his mouth open, holding the camera in his outstretched hands.

'Oh!' he mumbled, poking his fingers somewhere upwards. For Zhanaidarov, who realised that trouble had struck, his soul left his body. The Scotsman was singing something, rasping in his own language to his dazed countrymen. 'What could have happened has already happened!' thought Zhanaidarov, and came to his senses. The sheepskin in Ashten's outstretched hands fluttered in the strong wind.

There was an incredible uproar around the statue. Everyone huddled around Zhanaidarov and demanded an answer: 'What is it? Why is the skin in the sculpture's hands moving? Maybe it was only an optical illusion? Or was it really the wind blowing the hide?

It was impossible to not answer these questions. But how and with what? Finding no answers, Zhanaidarov looked expressively at the secretary. He looked at the instructors around him. Nobody knows how the situation would have ended if the head of the cattle breeding department, the one who had suggested putting Ashten on the plinth, had not come to his aid.

'This is a find by our sculptors,' he said suddenly, raising his eyes to the statue. They decided that if the skin in the tanner's hands were made of plaster or cast in bronze, it would not look good and would be unoriginal. If they gave him a natural skin, a natural hide, it would be much more interesting. We have a dashing collection of such skins here. The workers of the plant change this skin every week and renew it. Such a decision by the sculpture's authors brings viewers one step closer to the truth of life.'

He spoke at a feverish pace, so much so that he probably didn't realise what he was saying.

But the guests were stunned, and did not take their stunned eyes off the wind-whipped skin in the hands of the bronze man. Such a simple and therefore ingenious solution by the sculptors shocked them, and they emitted whole platoons of words in praise of the designers, claiming that hardly anywhere else could an artist have shown such ingenuity. At the moment when the guests again raised their heads upwards, then, as Ashten's fingertips had become stiff, the sheepskin, under every successive rush of wind, was torn from his hands and, swaying and whirling in the air, came down smoothly just before the Englishmen.

They parted and stared with some trepidation at the fallen rocks of genius.

'You dog, couldn't you have been patient a little longer!' reproved Zhanaidarov to Ashten without raising his eyes. Neither the guests nor the interpreter understood what he said and began to interrogate.

An explanation was given by the secretary for ideology:

'He expresses embarrassment to the guests about what has happened. It has never happened before; it seems the workmen didn't attach the hide very firmly this time.'

Here the Scotsman turned to the interpreter and delivered a long monologue. The interpreter was silent, shrugging his shoulders, then approached Zhanaidarov:

'He says: you change this skin every week anyway. This one suddenly fell out of the statue's hands. Can't I buy it as a souvenir? He promises to pay five hundred pounds sterling. How do you feel about that?'

Zhanaidarov, who with all his gut felt that disaster was approaching by the minute, rubbed his fingers against each other in his pocket, sweating with excitement.

'Let him take it for free,' he said, and smiled as if to acknowledge his generosity.

The Scotsman, who did not seem to understand a word of Russian before, understood and exclaimed:

'Ooh, that's some good Russian!'

'He is a Kazakh, not a Russian,' the interpreter laughingly corrected.

'Yeah, ta, ta! Cossack!' the Scotsman laughed, too. 'Free is good! Scotsman lubits free!'

Everyone laughed in unison and then, from up high, Ashten gave a short hiss:

'Come on, it's freezing.'

The words were spoken so quickly that not only the foreigners but even Ashten's compatriots did not immediately realise where the voice was coming from. However, everyone, especially the English, realised that there was a sharp sound in the air, not even a sound, but a whole sentence in the local language, and immediately their laughter was cut short.

They began to look around as if someone had lightly rubbed them on the tip of their ears, but finding nothing and no one suspicious, they did not ask about anything.

For the thousandth time the Scotsman was thankful for the dry lamb hide that had lain in Ashten's barn for forty years. He wrapped it with the utmost care and put it in a bag with the big letters 'Adidas' on the sides.

The foreigners, despite the rather late hour, were not about to leave the unfortunate square, where a cold Ashten was still standing. In addition, the leader of the delegation, a lanky Englishman, was about to make another speech. He said that they were extremely happy to see with their own eyes this unique statue, a statue found nowhere else in the world, and that this visit would remain in their memory as the brightest one that greatly enriched their spiritual life. After him the Englishman, who was really Scottish, took the floor. He reported that they were in excellent spirits, that they would speak at length of this trip when they returned home, that the piece of hide which had fallen from the statue would henceforth be preserved in the British Museum and would thus become a national treasure, and confessed that he would gain at most ten thousand pounds by reselling the hide to the museum, as he had intended to do before. He even took some notes out of his pocket, but our people, brought up on morals different from theirs, which put morality and creation first, and money only in fifth or sixth place, immediately shoved the guest's pounds back into his purse. Just then there was a sharp sound like a clap, 'Khap!' The foreigners were once again confused. But to question them about anything was seen as inappropriate. Whether the cry came from the heavens or the ground, no one could make it out either.

Here again, the head of the propaganda department felt the advantage of the widespread bilingualism in the republic. He pretended to be explaining something to the first secretary of the district committee while in Kazakh he spoke words meant for a different ear:

'Hey, Ashten! You can see they're not leaving, they're all admiring you. Five more minutes and we'll have them out of here.' There came a groan or a gnashing of teeth from the statue. 'Hey, be still!' The head of the department looked under his feet. 'We don't want any more scandals from you.'

The secretary for ideology, after asking the interpreter for the name of the head of the delegation, addressed him:

'Mr. Conrad!' he turned round sharply.

'Excuse me, but we are expected!' The secretary tapped his finger on the clock face.

'Oh, ta, ta! Nato, nato!' he retorted and spoke in English, addressing his compatriots.

After five or six minutes, the square with the statue was empty. When the noise died down and the guests disappeared around the corner, Ashten jumped down from the plinth and, shaking off the snow, swore at the delegation and its attendants, everyone from the foreigners to his own countrymen. As a result of having to stand motionless for more than half an hour, every muscle in Ashten's body was twisted and his back ached as if it had been shot. Jumping down from the plinth, Ashten took the rest of the Sary-Agach out of his pocket and tipped it down himself.

***

When most of the late-night members of the delegation had settled down and gone to bed, there was a chilling cry in the room where the Scotsman and Mr Conrad, the head of the delegation, were staying. Conrad jumped out of bed and asked his roommate what had happened. It turned out that he had left his Adidas bag with the priceless gift of a sheepskin from the statue on a bench in the park. Conrad got up and woke the interpreter in the next room and explained what was going on. He said that the square with the statue was not far from the hotel and one had to walk straight ahead towards the huge mill building on his right. He was prepared to go along if necessary, but the Scotsman told him not to worry, he could find his way. He hurriedly got dressed and left the hotel.

It might take fifteen minutes at the most to get there and back, but half an hour had passed and Jones was still gone. The interpreter regretted letting him go alone. He went back to Conrad, saying, 'Well, Jones is still missing…'

All the members of the English delegation were already on their feet. The interpreter and Conrad had thrown on their coats and were about to go in search of them when Jones appeared, soaked, tired and dejected, mud splattered up to his bald head.

'I couldn't find it,' he blurted out, out of breath.

'How could you not find it?'

'I must have got lost.

'My God,' the interpreter exclaimed, 'You don't want to get lost here. You go straight through two streets and you can see the factory. Did you see it?'

'Yes.'

'Well, how come you didn't see the statue that stands in front of the mill?'

'No,' Jones assured, his eyes widening with horror. 'There was no statue.'

'What are you talking about? How is there no statue?'

'That's how it is. The factory is there, but there is no statue.'

'Ah,' laughed the interpreter. 'You must be on the wrong side of the mill. Come on, you two, let's go and have a look.'

When they approached the square in front of the factory, they stopped dead in their tracks, unable to believe their eyes. Everything was there: the plinth, the flowers, the floodlights in the bushes, but the figure of the tanner itself was not there. The interpreter and the foreigner looked at each other in bewilderment. Then, as if on cue, they rubbed their eyes and stared again at the spot where the statue had stood just an hour before.

'Oh!' shouted the Scotsman to the translator from Moscow, shaking his head puzzledly.

'It is very possible, sir! It happens all too often in this country. You must have heard about the theft of the Liverpool Railway Bridge. In one night alone…'

'Yes, I have,' the interpreter replied. 'It was in the papers.'

'And what is your statue compared to a railway bridge! It's almost like a puppet you can slip into your pocket and carry away. It's a mistake not to put guards around such a rare statue. It's even more irresponsible! Besides, the floodlights are all out. There's an empty bottle, it smells of vodka. So the thieves drank it here...!'

They went back to the hotel. It turned out that some old woman in plaid from the same delegation had already called the district committee and got everyone up on their feet. Soon Zhanaidarov and the secretary for ideology appeared in the hotel lobby. After explaining to them what was the matter, they, yawning, answered:

'There is no such thing.'

'Why is it impossible? Mr. Translator and I have just come from there. No statue, no bag.'

Zhanaidarov, still at home, found out what was causing the commotion in the camp of the British and took measures: the same instructors went to Ashten, to persuade him to return to his place, saying that it was not raining or snowing, it was warm and he could stay there for another ten or fifteen minutes.

The phone rang. The instructors reported that all was well.

'Well, let's go. Let's see,' Zhanaidarov invited the Englishmen along with him. 'It's not just the statue, the money will be lying on the road, no one will bend down to take it.'

When they approached the square in a noisy crowd, they saw a statue holding a new sheepskin in its outstretched hands.

'You see, the statue is in place. No one has even thought of stealing it. And the workers at the plant have already managed to put a new skin in his hands,' announced Zhanaidarov in a nonchalant tone, ostensibly wiping his eyes.

Jones and the interpreter clutched their hearts and stopped, swaying. As they got into the car and drove off, the ideology secretary, head back, turned to Ashten:

'Hey, Ashten, give the bag back to the foreigner. Nobody could have taken it but you. Give it back, don't embarrass the whole neighbourhood.

'My son has been dreaming of an Adidas bag for months now.

'Tomorrow I'll get you not one but two of these bags from the warehouse. Give this one back.'

''I was going to take it with me, but when my wife opened it, she saw an old lambskin and threw it out to the dogs.'

'Use the one in your hand. There must not be any marks on that hide.'

'Still, we should have taken £500 from him…'

He shook himself off, took the bag that hung on the post supporting the chain-link fence around the plinth, slipped a lambskin into it and handed it to the secretary.

'You have no use for English pounds, Ashten. All the shops where you could sell foreign currency are now closed. You can only buy with Soviet money. Understand? Now go home. And don't take a step out of the house without our permission. You never know what else these foreigners will think of.'

Ashten staggered back to his room, and the secretary staggered towards the hotel with his Adidas bag.

Zhanaidarov was preparing to take the foreign guests to the *jailau* when the red telephone rang again.

'Zhanaidarov speaking,' he picked up impatiently. 'What?!' he covered his eyes and was silent for a while. 'From Italy? When? Tomorrow...? Ugh! Well ok, we are waiting...'

He hung up and sat still for a long time, unable to come to his senses. 'He's a strange man,' he thought reproachfully of the first secretary of the district committee. 'Did he tell the whole world that a statue of a leather tanner had been unveiled? He had to make such a fuss about that damn statue! The English have barely been dealt with, and now the Italians are coming. They probably drank the advance, and now they're looking for a new order... And we don't care about ours...'

After seeing the English off, Zhanaidarov breathed a sigh of relief. Now the Bulgarians would be welcomed and seen off too... And after that he firmly decided not to have anyone else: he would say that the plinth had a crack in it. Better that than to be exposed for such a shameful fabrication.

The day before, when the Italian delegation arrived, it had been a warm day. However, fearing the eyes of local visitors, it was decided to show the Ashten statue at night…

As the night's darkness thickened and the people in the houses sat down to dinner, the secretary of ideology, taking four or five guests with him, arrived in the square in front of the mill. Ashten stood as if cast in steel, proud and motionless, holding a lamb's hide high in his hands. Not like the last time.' He must have gained experience, seemingly unmoved even if delegations from not only the socialist countries, but all the capitalist countries were to arrive.

At the sight of such an original statue, the Italian guests opened their mouths in amazement and squeezed their eyes shut in delight. When one of them opened his eyes, he saw something gleaming in the spotlight shining from below in the middle part of the worker's figure. He took a closer look and realised that it was the neck of an ordinary quatroon, sticking out of the pocket of the dirty sweatshirt of a sculpted hero, and was dumbfounded. After blinking for a while, he poked his elbow at a fellow delegate standing nearby and pointed at the neck of the bottle with his eyes. Hearing a suspicious whisper among members of the delegation, the secretary of ideology, without lifting his head, followed with his eyes where their gazes were directed and saw what they had seen. His heart shivered. As had been agreed beforehand, he beckoned to one of the instructors and began to scurry out of the crowd, trying to go unnoticed.

In two or three minutes the searchlights should have gone out, but they continued to shine brightly, as if to say, 'Look, look!' The secretary of ideology immediately sent another instructor to follow. And then the Bulgarian brothers, one by one, began to ask what it was that was shining in the pocket of the statue. The secretary replied that it was the first time he had ever seen such a thing, that it had snowed yesterday and that it was the ice which glistened in the light.

It turned out that there was a burnout in the electrical panel. While the two instructors searched for the electrician in the booth and demanded that the spotlights be turned off immediately, because that was the order from on high, the electrician replied: 'It takes at least twenty minutes, if not a whole hour, to repair the unit in the electric panel.' 'No, it has to be right away, five minutes at the most!' the instructors almost pleaded. 'Then there's only one thing to do,' the fitter said with a yawn. 'Connect one phase to the other and then the floodlights will burn out.' 'Come on!' They said to him, 'Let them blow up, as long as they don't burn out! Hurry up!'

Having given such an instruction, the two instructors ran to the site, knowing that Atashbayev was there in an agitated state.

As they ran towards the square, six floodlights went off one by one and it went pitch black.

'Well done!' praised Atashbayev, patting the panting instructors on the back. 'What speed! And now let's hurry up and get the guests out of here!'

Half an hour later they were noisily entering the hotel with their guests.

Zhanaidarov, having heard about the emergency in the square near the tannery and its successful resolution, sank back in his chair and stretched out to relax. After a while he suddenly burst out laughing loudly, and startled the secretary enough to make him jump out of his seat. He opened his mouth several times to ask 'What is wrong with you?', but Zhanaidarov kept on laughing. Then he sank back into his chair and waited patiently for the secretary to stop his wild laughter.

Soon, Zhanaidarov, still laughing, said:

'You said it was frozen ice, didn't you?' Without

waiting for an answer, he laughed again. 'Ice! In the pocket of the statue! What ice can there be now, look at the barometer! It is nine degrees above zero. And you're talking about ice! Hahaha! Did they believe you?'

Only now was Atashbayev's heart in the right place.

'I don't know,' he replied cheerfully, 'But at that moment I had to say something, to distract their attention.'

'Ah, Ashten, Ashten! Would a half an hour of standing on a plinth kill him without that damned vodka? No, we must take it with us! He's got some nerve. You don't say a word to him now and he still replies rudely. He'll drive us to our grave.'

The head of the propaganda department entered the office.

'Suyunshi! The sculptors are here!' he announced loudly. The two secretaries jumped up from their seats.

'Really?'

'Yes,' assured the chief propagandist. 'They just called from Alma-Ata. They told us to get a crane and workers ready. They said they will install it tomorrow.'

'Ugh, finally! Thank God! It's all over,' said Zhanaidarov with a deep sigh. 'Put everything else aside, just take care of the statue.'

A week later the statue of the first leather tanner

was officially unveiled and the locals could finally admire the sculpture, which had become famous long before it appeared in the square. Witnesses have claimed, with a chuckle, that the worker on the plinth looks identical to Ashten: that if you placed them side by side you wouldn't be able to tell one from the other. However, the arrival of his plaster counterpart did not cheer Ashten up. No one needed him now. But evil tongues claim that a bottle of Sary-Agach is still delivered to him every three days, so that he won't divulge the secret of how he became Ashten the Statue. People think the nickname comes from his resemblance to the statue. He knows the truth, but he won't tell. Until...

THE CONFRONTATION

The denouement between Yerezhep and Yelemes happened on the seventh of August in the year one thousand nine hundred and eighty-six. Only on the face of it did it begin suddenly. In reality, the fight could reasonably have started at any minute of the day or night in recent years. Circumstances, as they sometimes do, just did not seem to be the right ones. Today they couldn't have come at a better time... Of course, Yerezhep was very unhappy that everything had happened on this particular day, but what could you do, as they say, you could not go against fate... Of course, every fight has its own history.

Having been involved in an accident two years ago, Yerezhep lost his front teeth. The upper and lower teeth. Without them, his mouth was no longer a mouth, but empty and black on the inside, like an abandoned wolf's den. With that 'mouth' Yerezhep lived for two years. Everything he could hear from his peers and children about his 'lair' he had heard a dozen times. But the mockery was nothing. What was unbearable was something else. In public he could not talk or eat at his own leisure. Laughing was out of the question. Of course he could have his teeth done, but usual ones did not suit him, and he had no money for gold ones. There was only one thing to do: to keep his mouth shut and work harder. Silently.

A year later, Yerezhep was among the foremost leaders of the state farm. And he was recorded as a speaker in the debates at the district conference. Five days before the event, the director of the state farm remembered that Yerezhep had no teeth and was horrified.

'It's a disgrace! What to do?!' he shrieked, shooting glances at the party leader and the workers' committee.

'We should call him in for a chat,' suggested the party leader.

'For a listen!' shouted the director.' A conversation is when two people are talking. But if he's going to lisp like that...!'

'They'll say there's no one on our state farm with all their teeth,' said the worker. 'They'll say we don't take care of public health services...'

'The health of the workers is your direct concern,' the director reminded the worker, meaningfully. 'We have to take urgent action! We cannot send him to the district with a mouth like that! The management will not understand anything about our successes!

'Maybe we should send someone who looks like him. I mean, like a double,' suggested the workman hesitantly, but after examining the director's gaze he suggested nothing further. The director was anxious to 'take urgent action'.

'We need to get his teeth put in immediately, at least in the next three days. Where is our dentist?'

'Gone. For an internship in Alma-Ata.'

'When will he be back?

'Well, he only left today. This morning.'

'Idiots!' The director looked fiercely at his comrades-in-arms. 'What a mess! Call in that Yerezhep, let's hear what he thinks about this.'

Fifteen minutes later the director's Volga took Yerezhep to his office. He entered the office and, as befits a senior worker, sat down on a chair.

'How are the preparations for the performance going?' the director asked. Yerezhep was silent.

'I'm asking you!' the director jumped out from behind the desk. 'How is the performance?'

Yerezhep shuddered, as if awoken from a bad

dream, and said: *Halaso.*

At that, the tip of his red tongue flashed and disappeared into the darkness of his mouth.

The leaders looked at each other as if they had just been informed of a terrible disaster.

All right, you'd better be quiet and listen,' the director sighed at length. 'There's a conference in three days where you have to speak. We'll help you with the speech, but what about this...?' he tapped his teeth with the nail of his index finger. 'Look, we don't have time to talk. I am going to make a call to the neighbouring state farm. Go there and have your teeth in place by tomorrow morning. Got it? That's it. Take my car and go!'

Yerezhep shook his head.

'What don't you understand?' The director was stunned. 'You don't want your teeth put in?!'

'I don't want iron ones,' said Yerezhep. 'I want gold ones…'

'There is currently no gold in the state farm's cash register for your mouth,' said the director. 'Go and get some teeth put in. Any teeth!'

Yerezhep rose from his chair and headed for the door, but the worker blocked his way.

'Where are you going?!' The director could hardly restrain himself from counting the rest of Yerezhep's teeth. 'Do you want to disgrace the state farm in the eyes of the district management?!'

'They'll put the iron ones in, and then you'll have to go to the authorities. I don't have time for that. I'll put the gold ones in right away!'

'Alright, alright,' he sank down exhausted in his chair. 'Put the gold ones in. When?'

'As soon as I get the money…'

'And when will you have it, my dear fellow?'

'Thikth munfs.'

'The conference is in three days' time,' said the director again. 'He doesn't have the time, he says! And what, we do?!'

'I understand,' Yerezhep stood with his head low, but was firm.

Only I don't have the money now...

'Your teeth are private property and the state farm will not pay for them. It's not in the budget!' The director yelled as loud as he could, letting off a stream of indignation. 'Borrow from someone…'

The director looked around the room with a heavy stare.

'Who will lend him the money?'

The party manager and the representative of the worker's committee, unable to grasp the meaning of the question, remained silent.

They jumped up at the same time, but the worker was more nimble and was the first to leave the office. Soon he was back, leading Yelemes, the driver of the car, by the hand. He followed the worker, not understanding anything, but with no apparent willingness, as if he felt that something unpleasant was about to happen to him.

The director did not hesitate to get down to business.

'How much did you get?'

'Four hundred and fifty…'

'How much do you need? 'The director looked at Yerezhep with hatred.

'Four hundred... Three for the teeth and a hundred for the mouth…'

'Listen, Yelemes... Give this man four hundred roubles. It's a loan, so to speak, at the request of the state farm administration... he's going to have his teeth put in!'

'And my wife?! 'Yelemes realised that his hunch was right. 'What will I tell her? And the children…'

'That's enough!' When the director realised there was a way out, he perked up. 'Give it back and that's it. You'll get your money in a month. I'm a witness! And don't argue, this case is political!'

Gold teeth could only be inserted in the district

centre, and the director personally took Yerezhep there, to make sure the money was used for its intended purpose, to listen to him speak at the conference, and, if all went well, to return home.

A year passed and Yerezhep still had not returned the money to Yelemes. Only three years later did he put four hundred roubles in an envelope, told his wife to set the table, and invited Yelemes and his wife to the house to make amends. During the meal, when the guests had quietened down and a suitable atmosphere prevailed, Yerezhep solemnly placed an envelope in front of the tractor driver, on which was written: 'Chimkent region, Bugensky district, state farm 'Karaspan', Bayzhansay branch, Yelemes Yestayevich Nuraliyev'.

Yelemes opened the envelope and, to everyone's surprise, immediately started counting the money. After counting it, he carefully folded the notes, put them back into the envelope and muttered:

'I won't take this.'

'Why not?! Yerezhep looked at his guest in amazement.

'It's not enough.'

'What's not enough?!'

'The money isn't enough. I won't take it.'

'It can't be! It's exactly four hundred!' Yerezhep,

flashing his golden teeth, started to count the money again, but Yelemes stopped him.

'Don't bother, there's four hundred there. But when you took money from me, one tooth cost fifty roubles, and and now it's a hundred.'

Yerezhep looked at his wife in confusion, but she was in need of help herself. Then he turned his gaze to Yelemes' wife. The wife sat stony-faced. Yerezhep was speechless.

'So what you're saying is... you think I owe you…'

'Exactly. You owe me eight hundred roubles. That's what you're going to pay me.'

'But I took four hundred from you…'

'You didn't just take it, you took it by force with the help of your superiors! I haven't forgotten how I was dragged into the office like a lamb to the slaughter. You'll give me 800.'

'What are you talking about?! What's it got to do with me? You were brought here by the workman…'

'It doesn't matter. Did you get your teeth put in with my money? Yes, with my money. Did your teeth go up in price? Yes, they went up! You should have given me the money right away, before the inflation. I won't take four hundred now. Only eight hundred.'

'What would you say if I spent it on something else? That hasn't gone up in price…'

'Then I would have taken four hundred. In short, you can be offended or not, but you'll either give me back eight hundred roubles or my teeth.'

'What do you mean, your teeth?!'

'It's very simple. Eight teeth!'

'I didn't put in eight, I put in six.' Yerezhep opened his mouth, presenting his teeth as proof. 'And I gave a hundred roubles to the dentist to do it quickly…'

'That's of no interest to me. It's up to you, either eight hundred roubles or eight gold teeth. I said…'

Yelemes rose from his chair, indicating that the meal was over. His wife began to get up from the table. But they stopped halfway through when Yerezhep began shouting.

'Hey, are you crazy?! I thought he was joking, and he...! What kind of a brain have you got that's so stupid? You're asking for your teeth back? Like hell I will! Here's your money, take it! If you don't want it, fine, that's all you're getting!'

Yerezhep threw the envelope in front of Yelemes, but he flung it back at him. The money scattered, one note falling into a bowl of cold tea. Yerezhep snatched it from the crockery in a lightning motion, slipped it into the envelope, and poked the envelope into the inside pocket of his jacket.

'Well, look, it's my job to offer. I've done my duty.

Now you'll never see that money again!' He was seething with righteous indignation. 'It's as if I had my teeth put in for nothing! You heard what I had to say at the conference, you politically illiterate...!'

'You don't confuse your teeth with your politics, got it?!' said Yelemes, hurt by the sting. 'Have you forgotten how you caused the accident? You were drunk, remember? I'll tell this to the right person and we'll watch you dance! We'll see who's literate then! And remember, those six teeth gleaming in your jaw are mine. I can knock them out at any time too. Gently supporting his wife under his arm, Yelemes left Yerezhep's house.

'Swindler! Cheat!' Yerezhep shouted after him. 'And you cooked meat for them?! Throw it to the dogs! Yes, only to the dogs!'

His wife, making it clear that no amount of resentment, not even Yerezhep's mortal grudge, would make her throw away the meat, pointedly and calmly remarked to him:

'Stop shouting at the whole village. You're a liar! I suspected the accident was caused by drunkenness, and that's how it turned out! I knew in my heart... You'll give him eight hundred roubles. Eight hundred, got it?!'

The rumour of this dinner spread quickly through

the village and the whole state farm went wild with laughter. But the louder the laughter, the fiercer the relationship between Yerezhep and Yelemes became. The villagers were looking forward to a fight and predicted it was coming... But contrary to these passionate expectations, everything ended quietly and peacefully. Amazed at the cleverness of Yelemes, the director thought that in case of an inquiry the story of Yerezhep's teeth could backfire on him too, and sent a district officer to see Yelemes. After two visits, Yelemes agreed to pay four hundred roubles and thus the threat to Yerezhep's teeth was averted.

But the resolution of the financial misunderstanding did nothing to change their relationship. Yelemes hated Yerezhep for applying administrative pressure when he borrowed money. Yerezhep accused Yelemes of taking advantage of the rise in the price of gold to extort him and, in addition, of blabbing the real cause of the accident to the whole village. Thus, their relationship crossed a line beyond which reconciliation was no longer possible.

Another wedding was in progress at the state farm. As is the custom on such occasions, there is an intricate and ornate subordination at the table, according to which the guests are seated from the place of honour in the red corner to the chair by the door according to the decreasing degree of authority and influence. For a Kazakh one of the unsolvable problems is his own place at a dastarkhan. Who will sit with whom, what will be put in front of whom, whose name will be mentioned more often (and whose less often) – all these questions have dignity riding on them, and during banquets these issues become as important as searching for peace in the Middle East...

At such a crowded feast, Yelemes was seated 'below' Yerezhep. This meant that from now on, Yerezhep would automatically be considered more respected than Yelemes. It meant that at the table Yerezhep would eat before Yelemes, drink tea before him and make a toast before him... At the dastarkhan everyone should know his place and position, but nevertheless there is an invisible inner confrontation of virtues. Such a confrontation – of course, masked by delicacy, kindness and generosity – immediately arose between Yerezhep and Yelemes from the very beginning of the meal.

It came to about two o'clock. In the old days that was enough time for a few scandals to erupt at the 'lower' end of the table and a couple of low-powered brawls outside the door. But this wedding did not serve alcohol, and for the whole two hours the guests, demonstrating excellent breeding and restraint, concentrated and drank tea, although none of them was thirsty. And so for these two hours Yelemes was playing on Yerezhep's nerves. It is known that tea at a dastarkhan is served, so to speak, from the bottom up – from the door to the most distinguished place. It means that Yelemes had to serve a tea bowl to Yerezhep, and the latter had to send it further, towards the most respected person... But every time it was Yerezhep's turn, the tractor driver gave it to somebody else with an innocent face, or, outrageous as it was, he put it in front of him. This was repeated every time for the entire two hours.... A second before giving the bowl directly to Yerezhep, Yelemes would start a very engaged conversation with someone, and seemingly for his own amusement he would put Yerezhep's bowl in front of him and even take a sip from it!

'Rascal!' Yerezhep shouted to himself. 'Like hell you're listening that attentively! You don't have enough brains for interesting conversations!' And Yerezhep snatched his bowl right out of Yelemes's hands as he brought it to his mouth, and with a clatter put it defiantly in front of him and hissed:

'What are you doing, giving the horses a drink? There are three pails in front of you!' Yelemes heard perfectly well about the horse, but he didn't even raise an eyebrow.

'I am a humble man,' he muttered through gritted teeth, keeping a nonchalant expression on his face. 'I've never had a horse. I wanted to get the donkey drunk, but you took the bowl yourself. And thank goodness…'

Yerezhep, savouring his tea, thought for a long time about the meaning of these words. While he guessed, he took a sip of tea from the bowl, but forgot to swallow it. 'Son of a bitch!' Yerezhep culturally wiped his mouth with his handkerchief, 'If we were somewhere else I would punch you!' Yelemes, finding no visible reaction on Yerezhep's part, leaned towards his ear.

'Do you know why Kazakhs need guts?'

'Why? What kind of stupid question is that? 'Yerezhep looked at the tractor driver as if he was mad.

'So they don't burn their arses when they drink hot tea.' The guests sitting around them roared deafeningly.

'Why aren't you laughing?' Yelemes asked. Yerezhep pursed his lips, showing great dignity.

'Your jokes wouldn't even make an idiot laugh…'

'Right. That's why you're not laughing…'

This implied that Yerezhep was an idiot... 'We should punch him,' Yerezhep warmed up to himself. 'No, a fight is inevitable. But in front of all the people!

In front of the director! So be it. Honour comes first! It's a shame, of course, but we'll have to fight. Although it would be better elsewhere, you can't offend the owners of the house...'

'Yeah, they've completely forgotten what a fight is these days. It's all quiet now,' one of the elders said dreamily.

'That's right.,' the second elder supported him.

'It's just like sitting in a cemetery,' the elder praised the wedding. 'Before, every dastarkhan was always fights, police...' He looked at the police officer nestled at the head of the table, as if he were a highly respected man.

'Yes, that's right,' the senior lieutenant said, and no one could tell whether there was more joy or regret in his voice.

'No fights, no other disturbances of public order,' the storekeeper interjected, glancing at the stubby neighbourhood officer. 'I wonder what you're going to do now?'

'We'll find something,' the police officer smiled meaningfully, to which the storekeeper reacted instantly.

'We should call the district,' he said to the director, 'and ask for a reduction in the number of district policemen on our state farm...'

The thought seemed so desirable that he laughed with pleasure, but soon stopped when he saw that he was laughing all alone.

Senior Lieutenant Seksenbayev listened to the laughter of the storekeeper and grinned again... The guests began to squirm in their seats, calming down after the storekeeper's joke, and all of them looked meek and gallant.

'What a bunch of goody-goodies,' Yerezhep said fiercely. 'And when you dig into each of them, they all have sins behind them... There, the policeman is sitting like a virgin in the bathhouse, and how about remembering his behaviour after my accident...!'

After the accident Yerezhep threw himself at the policeman's feet and started complaining that he had hit not a person but a pole, which was in the middle of nowhere, and that therefore the case could be hushed up without any fear. But Mr. Seksenbayev was adamant: he silently wrote up a report of what happened to Yerezhep, put it into a file, and left. Having forgotten about the broken teeth, Yerezhep wandered to the policeman's house, but he would not let him in even to the yard. In the evening Yerezhep paid another visit to the district police officer, but he was not at home. 'He has gone to the district,' muttered the wife of the senior lieutenant. Yerezhep clutched his head. 'That's it, he's gone. He'll report, they'll record it, they'll put him in jail.' And at that moment it dawned on Yerezhep: why was the neighbourhood policeman going to the district at night...? Just then, he saw the policeman's five-year-old daughter looking for a cat on the porch. Yerezhep took three crisp roubles from his pocket and handed them to the girl.

'Tell me where your daddy went and I'll give you some money. You can use it to buy gum tomorrow.'

'Over there,' the girl pointed to the grain store with one hand and grabbed the money with the other. He got on the cart and drove off.

Yerezhep sat down in the place where the road was closest to the old cemetery. After an hour in the night there was the creaking of a cart. The divisional guard himself remained silent – apparently it was not very much fun to drive past the cemetery at night, and meeting people was not something he was very keen on doing. As the carriage drew nearer, Yerezhep jumped out onto the road and shouted:

'Name!

'Sex... Sex...' Falling to the bottom of the donkey cart, the district officer held back the frightened donkey with all his might.

'What kind of sex?!' Yerezhep shouted. 'Speak when you arc spoken to!'

'Sex... Seksenbayev..'.

'How many bags are you carrying?'

'Eleven…'

'So, citizen Seksenbayev...' Yerezhep lowered his voice, but did not change his official tone. 'Your crime is even worse than mine. So, either you tear up all the paperwork about my accident, or I will go to the police station myself. Good night!'

Now this Seksenbayev was sitting behind the dastarkhan with his eyes downcast, as if there was no man on earth more crystalline and humble... 'And this storekeeper…' Yerezhep blew his nose noisily… he knew a thing or two about that one... 'The hell with them, truly, only babies are innocent.'

It was the seventh day of August in the year one thousand nine hundred and eighty-six... The last week was marked in Yerezhep's house by a rare, lyrical mood – his wife's younger sister and her friend, students of the Moscow Schepkin Theatre School, had come to visit them! Both of them were slim, beautiful and smiling, as if they had come out of the poster that hung on the wall of the state farm club.

Waiting for the dust to settle and the cooler weather to settle on the main street, they would go out for a walk in the village, and it was impossible to find anyone indifferent to these two figures, wrapped in jeans and tight-fitting blouses. The sedate inhabitants of the village had a certain aesthetic interest in the girls, while younger people, and especially the bachelors, looked at them in a fundamentally different way. The most hardened-minded misogynists headed for Yerezhep Street, though their business was in the opposite direction. Yerezhep's house became a magnet that attracted all the male population of the village, except old men of course, to its porch. For these days, the man of the house returned from work without any delay, took a shower (which he had never done before), and cologned himself from head to toe, in an attempt to look urbane. Then he took the girls under his arm and led them to the club. Oh, how Yerezhep felt in those moments! It was an impossible dream even for the most dapper young men of the village to approach some students from the Schepkin drama school, but Yerezhep, just a driver of an old dump truck, with fuel oil under his nails, held the girls, both at once, under his arms and led them wherever he wanted! If only that! There were moments when the girls, bursting with laughter, rested their heads affectionately on Yerezhep's shoulders... Yes, the Providence of the Creator works in mysterious ways: one man gets everything and the other gets nothing.

The peculiarity of men in our village, as in all the villages on the planet, is that they do not forgive the success of their own kind in front of a beautiful woman. Yelemes and Yerezhep, who grew up in a village where they had never known anything about Schepkin's school or Schepkin himself, nevertheless had a good understanding of the intricacies of the relationship between a man and a woman and how to make an opponent angry. For the whole week Yerezhep rejoiced. Every evening he led the girls under his arms past Yelemes' house, feeling how he was ruining and humiliating his mortal enemy every time.

So today the girls, who had been the jewels of the village for a whole week, got ready for their journey home. It was decided that Yerezhep would take them to the intercity bus that passes the state farm to Chimkent, and from there they would go by plane to Moscow. What a life, thought Yerezhep, feeling sorry for himself. 'And how do I live? Bickering with Yelemes, driving dung on a dump truck.... Now they're moving on, back to their Schepkin school...!'

For the farewell, Yerezhep borrowed a blue Zhiguli from the shepherd Metesh. He could not have driven the girls in his dump truck! But the neighbour's Zhiguli was not looking good either – the side windows had long since fallen through the doors, and the old treads were gleaming like a thoroughly shaved bald spot.

'You watch out,' said Metesh. 'If the traffic police catch me they'll take my car away. I don't even go out of the gate with these treads.'

For the first half of the day, Yerezhep scrubbed the Zhiguli, especially the interior of the car in which Metesh had recently taken two rams into town to sell. In the evening he opened the doors with a broad gesture, seating the girls in the back and his wife beside him. Almost the whole village came out to see the students off. The girls were moved by this attention and even shed a few tears. It was all so touching...

But as soon as he crossed the village, he saw a Belarus tractor with a trailer far ahead. The tractor was rushing towards the sun, wiggling its trailer playfully. There was no doubt that Yelemes was sitting at the wheel. The next second Yerezhep's mouth fell open in amazement... The Belarus, instead of driving on the left side of the road as it should, started to take the right side, presumably to let the dust fall on the Zhiguli. Yerezhep, pulling over to the side of the road, shut off the engine and started fumbling with his hands on the doors in search of the window lift handles. But neither windows nor the handles for them were known to be in the car. Yelemes made a sharp turn around the car, and dashed away from the Zhiguli at an arm's length... The interior was instantly filled in, as if a sack of cement had been poured into it. Yerezhep turned around, but there was also a thick wall of dust behind him.

That was the limit. It was no longer possible to live like this. As soon as the dust had settled, Yerezhep ran after the tractor. Despite the entreaties of his wife and girls, he drove the Zhiguli after enemy number one. The Zhiguli was easy to catch up with. Yelemes leaned out of the cab and smilingly asked:

'Has something happened?

Yerezhep signalled for him to get off the tractor. Yelemes seemed to be waiting for this. He instantly jumped down and stood in front of Yerezhep with a beaming smile on his face. Yerezhep had been thinking for years about how to strike if the last argument in their relationship was with fists, and so he struck quickly and in cold blood. Apparently Yelemes wasted no time either, for his fist almost simultaneously jammed into Yerezhep's cheekbone.

By the time the women reached the tractor, Yelemes and Yerezhep had managed to grab onto each other properly. The blows of both were perfectly accurate, and by the time the women arrived to separate them, both were standing with their eyes misted over. Seksenbayev emerged from the cloud of dust and things took a turn for the worse. The dust, the fight, the police – all this was not for the weak hearts of the girls, and their loud crying was added to everything else. But it was the tears of the students of the Schepkin school that caused Yelemes to feel deeply satisfied; he believed they were only crying because they had seen him hit Yerezhep.

'You can draw up ten reports on me, but don't detain me now,' said a frowning Yerezhep. 'The plane will not wait.'

The police officer released the passengers of the Zhiguli and concentrated on writing up the incident in the report.

'He's a good fighter,' said Yelemes, looking at the car. 'I should have had a little talk with him a long time ago, he walks like a turkey…'

'Here, sign here,' Seksenbayev handed a pen to Yelemes, who was already settling into the tractor cab.

'What do I sign?

'It's about fighting and breaking traffic laws.'

Yelemes looked thoughtfully at the paper and pen handed to him.

'Look, it wasn't a fight. It was a…'

'What was it then, a kiss? I saw it all, now sign it!'

'It wasn't a fight! You wouldn't understand!' He looked down at his feet and saw two of his teeth.

'That's it,' said Yelemes, carefully picking up his property, lost forever, from the dust. 'Now, Comrade Seksenbayev, the confrontation is over.'

'What's happened?!' the policeman asked with a grimace of anguish on his face. He was trying to imagine what a man who had just had two teeth knocked out must be going through.

'I'm saying, our confrontation is over... ' Here Yelemes stammered. He realised that he could not pronounce that beautiful foreign word 'Confrontation' as it was intended, because he could not make the 'r' sound.

Yerezhep, learning of Yelemes' knocked-out teeth, sent a note to him informing him that he was ready to pay for the insertion of both gold teeth at the new price and immediately return the eight hundred roubles as requested by Yelemes. It is said that on receiving this dispatch, Yelemes almost burned with shame.

1989

SKYSCRAPERS OF SOCIALISM

Whatever resolution was adopted in Moscow, as a rule, it was immediately reacted to in Almaty. It just so happened that from the first days of Soviet power, the decisions of numerous congresses and plenums, of which there were many, came flying over Russian villages and territories of other republics, without stopping once in the expanses of the state, ending up here to hastily be put into practice right away. Russian villages and republics did not have time to really hear about these decisions, and our Kazakhs, having rolled up their sleeves, were already implementing them. It is known, after all, whoever starts first is the first to finish, while the Russian villages and other republics were digesting what they had heard, slowly getting down to business, others asked themselves what they had heard, scratching their heads, meanwhile Kazakhstan was already reporting to the centre about the completion of their tasks, rubbing their hands in impatience, thinking about when they will be able to start implementing the new resolution.

One of the next, most important political decisions was the blurring on the line between the city and the countryside. As soon as the decision of the authorities reached Almaty, first - regional centres, then - districts, then - villages, the local authorities of which, accustomed not to shelve the decrees of high-ranking party leadership, immediately set to work. "But how, how can we blur the line between the city and countryside? And what are the differences between them? What needs to be done to eliminate these differences successfully and quickly?" These were the questions that the authorities in many districts of Kazakhstan puzzled over, holding meetings, studying the opinion of the conscious, informed activists.

We do not know how these issues were resolved in other places, but in the 'Socialism' department of the notorious collective farm of 'Communism', they concluded that the main difference between the city and the aul is connected by the presence or lack thereof multi-storey buildings. "What makes a city, a city? There are multi-storey buildings. What makes an aul an aul? These are one-story huts. If we demolish these huts and build high-rise buildings instead of them, then the main difference between the city and the village will disappear." Pashat Barakatov, head of the department, summed it up like this. "Thus, high-rise buildings will appear in the village, they will be our skyscrapers, that is, the heights of 'Socialism'." Pashat enjoyed well-deserved prestige, not only in the department, but throughout the collective farm. According to some people, Barakatov was once a step away from being enrolled in the Timiryazev Agricultural Academy in Moscow. He was aware of the current politics; he read newspapers and even had a knowledge of literary fiction. Last year, Pashat bought Ernest Hemingway's novel 'Farewell to Arms' in the village shop. At a time when the people in the village had not only never heard of such a writer, but could not even pronounce his name in syllables, he amazed many by exclaiming in public: "Oh, did Hemingway's works really come to our store?" People's jaws dropped in surprise. The management and the general meeting of the collective farm, taking Pashat's proposal as a basis, adopted a resolution as an experiment to build two multi-storey buildings in the "Socialism" department. The meeting instructed the foreman of the department, Sepentai, to go to the regional centre in order to obtain technical passports from the builders, the drawings of multi-storey buildings and to calculate construction costs at average prices.

"This order is unbearable for one person, let the manager of the department, Barakatov, take part," was an amendment Sepentai had made, at first Pashat mercilessly criticized him, then the chairman of the collective farm scolded him. "It is unusual for a communist to run away from difficulties. What does the party charter say about this? You are avoiding responsibility," they said. Since two people had expressed their opinion, what was there left for the rest to do? The activists harshly condemned Sepentai, and there were those who offered to take his party card away from him, and to exclude him from the collective farm and drive him out. The head of the sheep insemination station, veterinarian Ospan, expressed regret that he had to work in the same team as that of such a duplicitous and cowardly communist. Twenty-one people took part in the meeting, all of them were Kazakhs, of course, they did not speak Russian, and if some could speak, then it was only at such a level where they would pronounce the word water as - 'uada'. Despite this, Ospan expressed his thoughts entirely in Russian. Since the speech was delivered in Russian, the meeting listened attentively to the speech of the veterinarian. They became convinced that Sepentai was a dishonest communist, that he is a reactionary element, looking for any opportunity to damage the cause of the developed socialism, that he is against the policy of destroying the distinction between city and village, against the general point of view that work for the good of socialism is creativity. At this meeting, Sepentai was forced to apologize in the meeting for his ideological apostasy and deviationism, he admitted his mistake, and promised to soon, no, immediately correct himself, and assured everyone that he would fulfil this important party assignment, no matter how difficult it may be, and, in general, follow all orders.

A simple majority voted with one vote to pardon him, with only one person abstaining.

The next day he left for the regional centre. Since Sepentai never crossed the threshold of such important institutions, he barely found the building of the Regional Construction Project, which is next to the Regional Project of Kazakhryba, after meeting the right person there with whom he could reinterpret. The people he found could not decide anything on their own. The fourth day was crowned with success: in a remote corner office where four dzhigits* were sitting, there

**dzhigit – nomadic horse riders from Central Asia and North Caucasus, usually distinguished by their courage, endurance and exceptional horse-riding ability*

was a man who said that he knew an architect in the 'Yuzhkazelevatormelsnabsbytstroy' organization who had a project of two high-rise buildings in his hands. And if Sepentai agrees, he can meet with this person for a conversation and persuade him to sell his projects at an affordable price in the name of communism to the Socialism department. Sepentai was beside himself with joy, he worked with the dzhigits from the office until he got his way.

For two days they negotiated with the architect from 'Yuzhkazelevatormelsnabsbytstroy'. The negotiations were held in a secluded place, in a city recreation park in the Aral restaurant on a lake island with a warm atmosphere, an atmosphere of complete mutual understanding.

A month later, the results of Sepentai's stay in the city began to appear. From the regional centre to the 'Socialism' department, cars with building materials poured in a stream, then the working people poured in; plasterers and masons, architects and bulldozer operators, surveyors and concrete workers. How was Sepentai to know that those drawings that were sold for twenty thousand rubles to the collective farm were projects that were gathering dust in a forgotten box of the institute: not accepted by the authorities, they were rejected at all levels.

A rumour spread throughout the region that the Socialism branch needed workers, and the unemployed rushed there from all sides. There were more and more people who went out onto the highway and raised their hand to stop a ride:

"My friend, where are you going?"

"Where are you heading to yourself?"

"To the 'Communism' collective farm. I've been stuck here for an hour, any longer and I'll cry, take me with you."

"Can't do, my car is faulty. Will it be alright if I take you to the 'Socialism' department instead?"

"Oh, that's it, that's where I need to go."

Not more than two weeks passed, and that small office was overflowing with visitors. Poor Pashat and Sepentai were dizzy - they did not know where to go from the onslaught of the people. Having entrusted the main work in the department to the linkers and foremen, they took care of the visitors completely. Having hired the right number of people, they sent the rest home. At first, they did not know how many workers would be needed to build two seven-story buildings. Like a flock in a paddock, the people were noisy, chattering, crowding in the room. Whom were they to leave alone, whom to send back - were the organizers lost, unable to resolve these issues?

"How many people do we need? Who do we leave from these restless devils?" Asked Pashat, ready to vent his anger on Sepentai. "How many workers, do you suppose, would be needed to build such houses in the city?"

"That's the city, and this here – it's the steppe. There is more equipment here than people, but even then, we only have one crane, three dump trucks, and that's it."

"I'm not asking you what we have and what we don't. Tell me, how many people do you need for one house?"

"I mean, except for the tech... hmmm..." Sepentai moved his lips, keeping the score. "Hmmm... back and forth, here and there... Twenty on the first floor, twenty-five on the second floor... third floor... fourth... fifth... One building needs one hundred and twenty people."

"Hey, we're not going to build five floors at the same time. First, we will build the first floor, then we will proceed to the second, is that not how it works? Or will your people lay bricks in the air?"

"Well, in reality... that is true, until the first floor is completed, you cannot proceed to the second, because the second floor is being built on the first."

"That's right, comrade foreman. If I don't explain everything, you yourself will never understand. So how many people do you need, in the end?"

"One head is good, two is better. Let's leave one hundred and fifty people, send the rest home. If it's too much, then we'll cut it down as needed."

"All right, get the teams! However, make sure to strictly observe the international composition of the workers." At this time, the old door jambs, on which the crowd peering inside pressed against, could not hold them any longer, they broke away from the adobe walls, and the door collapsed right into the office. The ten people who were about to enter first flew head over heels over the threshold onto the floor, crushing and breaking the straw hats of some. Two or three of the poor fellows were able to get out of the heap and rushed to the authorities, but on the way, they were overcome by timidity, and they stopped halfway. Sepentai looked sternly at the dark-haired, thin dzhigit who was floundering under a pile of bodies, and asked:

"What's your last name?"

"Kamysbaev."

"What's your speciality?"

"I'm a bricklayer."

"Your nationality?"

"Konyrat."

"I'm not asking where you're from, but what nationality you are."

"Kazakh... But I'm only asking because I heard that you are also from Konyrat..."

"Oh, these Kazakhs! Even when being crushed by a crowd, they will still try to divide into tribes. Okay, accepted. Well, what about you... sir, what is your last name?" Sepentai shifted his gaze to the bald guy, who was lying on top of the heap.

"Kopbergenov."

"Speciality?"

"Bricklayer."

"Nationality?"

"Kazakh. I'm also a Konyrat..."

"He's lying, he's a Naiman!" Blurted out a pockmarked dzhigit with protruding ears, floundering nearby.

"Kazakh, Kazakh," Sepentai thought, eyes darting from one man to another. "Kazakh again. It would be nice if there was a Russian. If everyone is a Kazakh, then..." Sepentai stopped himself and sighed.

"Are there any Russians among you?" The crowd was silent. "Are there Russian masons among you?" Shouted Sepentai into the corridor that was buzzing like a beehive.

"There is!" Answered some bright dzhigit in a

sombrero from the crowd.

"What's your last name?"

"Bekturov."

"Bekturov? What kind of Russian are you?"

"My father's name was Victor, when they wrote the metric, the Kazakhs wrote Bektur instead of Victor."

"Eh, that sounds quite farfetched, I don't believe it. Well, whatever, Satan will deal with you later, accepted, go on!"

While Sepentai was calling on all the nationalities living in Kazakhstan, the evening came. Exhausted from fatigue, he said to Pashat:

"That one time in the newspaper it read that representatives of one hundred and thirty nationalities live in friendship and harmony in Kazakhstan. I got one hundred twenty-seven here today. Where can we find the remaining three? Who are these peoples?"

"Was there a Kurd?"

"Yes."

"Was there a Nogai?

"Yep."

"And Chinese?"

"Those as well."

"What about the Shurshits?"

"Shurshits? No, I don't think we had any of

those... What kind of nation is it?"

"How am I supposed to know what kind of nation it is. We just hear the people always mention them: 'Shurshits this, Shurshits that.'"

"Alright, I'll try asking," he looked at the people left in the corridor, and asked:

"Are there any Shurshits?"

"No."

"Are there at least any Pashtos?"

"No. They live in Afghanistan."

"Eh, we desperately need some Shurshits, Pashtos... And what about you, who are you?"

"What do you mean who? We're Kazakhs."

"Eh, we don't need Kazakhs. You can go."

"Oh god! Perhaps you think that a house built by the Kazakhs will fall? Wherever we go, us Kazakhs are turned away from the gate. Where do we go now, how do we live?"

"That is none of our business. If you want to help, go to the end of world will you! And whilst you're there, bring us a Shurshit, or at the very least an Eskimo."

"Oh god, what if we can't find any, are we to just - die?"

"Go and find them then, find them!"

No matter how many times the bosses called out, neither Shurshits, nor Eskimos, nor Pashtos responded from the crowd. They once again carefully checked the list, and, making sure that they hadn't missed anything on there, they looked at each other.

"What do we do now?" Pashat asked sadly. Sepentai thought for a long time.

"What if we do this?" He whispered. "We will add eight nationalities, which were not here today, from the list of the remaining Kazakhs: We will write down one as a Pashto, the other as a Shurshit. What else is there for the unemployed to do – they'll definitely agree. And we will agree with them, we will explain to them, and if the inspectors become interested, they will name the nationalities that we assign to them."

"What if their looks don't match?"

"Who cares about their looks? Do you think anyone will really bother examining the appearance of all these working people? When they find themselves covered in dust and dirt at work, they will all have the same appearance as that of any proletariat."

"Pashat gazed at Sepentai for some time."

"What a brilliant, expeditious idea!" he said, smiling happily. "Well done, Sepentai! Your head does work it seems. Though only from time to time."

And Pashat, as if he was being tickled, giggled effusively in a thin voice. Then he coughed brusquely, masking his laughter.

"Come on, get to work," he said. "However, do not write whatever comes into your head, but choose the appearance that suits the desired nation."

"Certainly. In truth, you can find an appearance suitable for any nearby nationality among the Kazakhs."

"This is true. Well, I'm going home, you finish the rest yourself," with these words, Pashat, pushing the people crowding in the corridor, went out into the street. Sepentai did not bother with this matter for long. He selected eight Kazakhs from the crowd, whose appearance, in his opinion, corresponded to the desired nationalities, then explained to them that if they agreed to the conditions, he would immediately apply them for work. None of the chosen Kazakhs wanted to miss the chance, and they chattered fervently from all sides:

"Oh god, do you really think we'll argue? If it comes to it, you can mark us down not only as Shurshits, but also as earthworms if needs be - we will be satisfied. It won't hurt us. And if someone in the future becomes interested in what nationality we are, we will answer as you instruct us. We'll just need to write it down, so we don't forget who we are.

A bit of time passed, and on the construction site of the 'Socialism' department of the 'Communism' collective farm, vigorous activity began to boil on the construction of the two seven-story houses. Even before the construction of the foundations, two banners were hung out on the border of the site. A lot of old banners were gathering dust in the storeroom of the department's office. Sepentai pulled out two of them by the shafts, scraped off the faded obsolete words, and began to write out new ones. Instead of the appeals: "Let's catch up and overtake America!" and "Let's contribute to the construction of communism in 1980!" He instead wrote: "We will eliminate the differences between the city and the village at an accelerated pace!" and "Thank you to the party for existing in the era of developed socialism!" Then he hoisted the banners on two tall poles so that the proclamations could be seen from afar. Pashat, the manager of the department, contacted the centre every Monday by radio to report that the construction of buildings was proceeding at a marvellously unprecedented pace, and if these rates were maintained, two buildings would be erected not in a year, but in five months. He reported that the 'Socialism' branch would again come to the forefront in the yearly report, having completed everything ahead of schedule regarding the instructions of the party and the government to eliminate the differences between the city and the aul.

Still, Pashat and Sepentai kept their word - five months flew by like dashing horses, and the villagers began to prepare for the move. During the move, both leaders vigilantly ensured that the settlers did not turn out to be representatives of only one nationality, they solved this important task with great skill. Mostly Kazakhs lived in their department, though there were five or six families of Russians, three Uzbek, two Azerbaijani, one Turkish, one Georgian, one Armenian, and for some unknown reason, one Kyzylbash family, who arrived from Iran last year, one Dungan and one Korean. First of all, Pashat gave appropriate orders to these nationalities, he recorded the rest of the Kazakhs as representatives of all other nations living in Kazakhstan, and set a date for the move. In total, the department consisted of eighty-four families, huge seven-story buildings swallowed up these families in one sitting. Only two or three old women remained in the one-story huts, who did not want to live on the floors, and a few peasants who did not want to part with their households and outbuildings.

On the day of the resettlement, the chairman of the collective farm and other leaders arrived from the centre, and a solemn meeting was held in the courtyard of the new buildings. At the rally, the manager Pashat Barakatov made a fiery speech. He said that such a thing as the construction of beautiful seven-story residential buildings in five months, and not in the year allotted for this, is only possible under the conditions of developed socialism, and that the working people of capitalist countries are not only deprived of such a prospect, but also are simply unable to dream up anything like it. He casually mixed the dignity of capitalism with dust and ashes. Blaming America, the flagship of the capitalist world, for all mortal sins, and exposing Reagan, the president of America, as a kind of scarecrow and laughingstock. At this time, an old man standing in the front row said to him:

"Hey, Pashat, my friend, you're getting quite prideful, you just said you're building two buildings in the vast steppe, right? If that's it, why do you need to bother the distant America, wouldn't it be better to start talking about the affairs of your own village?"

Pashat immediately lost his temper, giving vent to the heap of anger:

"Who said that? Aksakal Meldesh, is that you? What, you didn't like my criticism of American imperialism? By twisting our words, maliciously, instead of being an example for young people, you demonstrate your extremist character every time. If you like America so much that you care about it, go there. We will not hold back malicious people for a minute. Or was the criticism that you received last time not enough?"

The people made a noise and turned towards the old fidget. And a lot of eyes burning with anger aimed for spoiling such a solemn event, and for trying to protect the distant America, which was the main enemy of the Socialism branch. There was a lot of truth in the words of Pashat, "Or was the criticism that you received to last time was not enough for you." Eight months earlier, Elder Meldesh bought two barrels of beer in the city on his pension, he brought it and distributed it free of charge to people near the collective farm club. A lot of people gathered near the club for free beer, in the end the stampede ended in a big fight. The old man's cart was broken, both barrels were crushed. The news of the incident reached the manager first, then the chairman of the collective farm. The chief, calling Meldesh into the office, asked:

"What is the meaning of this? Why are you disturbing the people?"

"Why is it my fault? I should only be at fault for deciding to treat people weary with work to free beer."

"Why?"

"Why not? You yourself say every day that under

communism everything should be free. I am already old, my age is approaching the limit, in order to see communism, which you talk so much about, I bought two barrels of beer for my two pensions and distributed them to the people. How was I to know that everything would end in a fight."

"Write!" The chairman said to his assistant, who was sitting next to him. "It's an order!"

Old Meldesh calmed down that day, having received a severe reprimand for disturbing the rest of the workers with his adventurous undertaking. Pasha reminded him exactly of this as he stood in front of the two buildings. Who knows how this situation would have developed further if the chairman of the collective farm had not reminded himself: "Okay, keep talking." Then Pashat, clearing his throat well, continued to read the prepared speech.

"Do not treat these two buildings that are in front of you, as if they are just homes. This is a model of the future, that is, a communist hostel. This is another outstanding achievement of the Soviet working people. These houses were built by representatives of all nationalities living in Kazakhstan, which is why they were completed seven months ahead of schedule. Today, multinational families are preparing to move into new homes. Not only Kazakhs, Russians, Ukrainians,

Tatars, Moldavians, Belarusians, but also representatives of all those other nationalities inhabiting Kazakhstan who took part in the construction and completion of these buildings. In particular, the Eskimo, Sagyntai Aibaltaev, the Pashto, Yergeshbay Sarmoldaev, and the Shurshit, Temirbek Sikymov, who have attracted attention with their hard work. And now about this celebratory event…"

The people murmured like a disturbed beehive. And only then Pashat realized that he had ruined everything with his thoughtless words, his face flushed with embarrassment and looked like a loaf that had just been taken out of the oven. It turns out that in the hassle he forgot to change the names of the people who he wrote down as having different nationalities.

"Hey, what kind of Eskimo is that? What kind of Shurshit?" Shouted the employees of the department, completely drowning out Sepentai. The dzhigits, whose names were called out by him, were there with their wives, children, and other relatives. And when one of them was called a Shurshit, another an Eskimo, and the third a Pashto, not to mention other people, their wives made an incredible noise.

"Hey, comrade opraulaish*!" Shouted the wife of the proclaimed Shurshit, Temirbek. "You will not disgrace my husband like that, not only is he not a

Shurshit, but he has never seen one in his entire life. He is a Kazakh! And not only is he a Kazakh, but his great-grandfathers are Otrar Konrats who fought with Genghis Khan, within the Konrats are the Kulshygash, within the Kulshygash are the Taz, within the Taz are the Bori, within the..."

"You shouldn't divide the Kazakhs into clans and tribes like that," the bewildered Pashat muttered out of place, biting his reddened lips. But then the wife of the Eskimo and the wife of the Pashto, raised their voices at once, and the solemn meeting turned into a noisy gathering. The chairman of the collective farm, realizing that this noise and uproar could last forever, stepped forward:

"Patience, comrades, patience!" He raised his hand. "Let the named comrades come forward, and we will see with our own eyes who they really are.

"They are the department workers we see every day. Why should they come forward?"

"Let them step forward anyway. Jzhigits, where are you? Come on, come forward!"

And when the Eskimo, Sagyntai, the Pashto, Ergeshbai and the Shurshit, Temirbek, came to the centre of the circle, the people burst into uncontrollable laughter.

**opraulaish – a corrupted/misleading manager]*

"Traitors!" One tipsy Jzhigit shook his fist at them. "They sold their nationality for thirty coins. But me, I stepped down, I said: 'Even if I have to be unemployed and collect beetles in the steppe for the rest of my life, I will still remain a Kazakh.' But now we saw with our own eyes what we heard! And I was wondering what this all was about, and now I know, why these men smiled so widely that their grin reached both of their ears when they left Sepentai's office!"

The assembly was noisy like a disturbed chicken coop. It is not known how this scandal, which crossed every boundary, would have ended if the chairman of the collective farm had not taken the reins of the government into his own hands.

"Stop making noise!" He got angry. "What are you talking about: 'You're a Shurshit, he's Shurshit?' Well, let them be, is it really hurting anyone? These days, every Soviet person is free to change to any nationality they want, when they feel like it."

He paused and waited, checking the effect of his words on the people, and when the noise subsided, he spoke calmly. In a pleading tone, he told the people about what was planned to improve the life of the villagers, then, after discussing the village, he switched to the domestic and foreign policy of the state, drawing general attention to the problem of national relations, finally, making sure that the people were slowly forgetting about the cause of the unrest and calming down, said to the newcomers: "I welcome you to your new home! May you live happily!" And then cut the prepared red ribbon with scissors.

Looking back at the ribbon in his hands, the huddled crowd poured into both seven-story buildings. And only then did the chairman of the collective farm, wiping his sweaty forehead, head towards his car. But before this, he understood, that he gave the people a reason to swear at their head of department, Barakatov, from the bottom of their hearts.

In the morning after breakfast, Pashat, the chairman of the collective farm, and Sepentai sat down to write a report to the district committee of the party:

"A Report to the District Committee of the CPSU,

The workers of the 'Socialism' department, branch of the 'Communist' collective farm, belonging to the Zhetisai region, are supporting the policy of the party and government to eliminate the differences between town and countryside in every way possible, they undertook an honourable obligation to build two seven-story buildings. According to the plan, it was envisaged that all construction work would be completed in full within a year. As a result of the heroic work of the residents of the branch and the involved workers, two sixty-four apartment buildings, that is, one hundred and twenty-eight apartments, were put into operation seven months ahead of schedule. Yesterday, that is, September 21st, 1981, the settlement of two new houses was fully completed. We assure you that in the future we are ready to strictly fulfil all the instructions of the party and the government.

Chairman of the Board of the Collective Farm Assembly,
B. Zhalmuratov.
Party Organization Secretary,
S. Kereybaev.
Manager of the ‘Socialism’ Department,
P. Barakatov.
September 22nd, 1981”

In order to immediately deliver the report, the secretary of the party organization, Kereybaev, urgently left for the regional centre. Having agreed to hold a meeting in the evening at the manager’s house to notify all responsible employees of the collective farm about the early completion of this important project, the three leaders dispersed. Pashat, who did not like to waste time, sat down at the radio in the collective farm board room and contacted the department and instructed them to slaughter and skin one heifer and two sheep by his return. Since the report had already been delivered to the district, it was decided that the party organizer, without stopping by the collective farm, would go directly to the department, and his family would stay with the rest.

At this time, the area in front of the two new houses turned into something resembling a cattle market. There was a frenzied roar, the bleating and lowing of cattle. In front of the house were crowds of horses, camels, donkey carts, heavily loaded “Zila”, “Kamaz” and “Belarus” vehicles parked side by side, caterpillar tractors, cotton harvesters. In short, whatever kind of equipment, livestock or product that someone on the collective farmer had, they put it in the yard. Everyone was only busy with the fact that they only had time to carry theirs loads from their vehicles to their houses. Since the move took place in hordes on the same day, the heated, sweaty people now and then collided at the entrances, it led to swearing, cursing and even assaults.

Only by midnight did the tired people more or less calm down, leaving unfinished business for the next day. In the new houses, however, as was the case for whole area, there was no home gas. Therefore, each of the new settlers, contriving who was good for what, looked for a way out of the situation in their own way. Some were content with tea from a thermos, some indulged their stomach with pieces of cold, boiled meat, some heated their food with electric stoves, and old Meldesh who lived with his old woman and grandson, well he boiled tea by setting a fire right on the balcony of their third floor. Many Kazakhs, accustomed to the spaciousness of their courtyards, with kindled fires that popped and sparked, built hearths on the site in front of the house. From an outside perspective, it seemed that these new houses were not objects of socialist brilliance, but sinking ships set on fire. People scurried between houses and hearths, some crushed down grain in a mortar, some pounded nails into their walls with a hammer, their fires burned with might and main on the balconies, the stoves in the yard scattered about their sheaves of sparks - in short, the seven-story communist dormitories whiled away their God-given days as they could.

Tomorrow these families would celebrate a housewarming event, and the residents of the houses, according to the traditions of one hundred and thirty nationalities living in Kazakhstan, will sing songs and dance from day till night. The people settled in these buildings were mainly chauffeurs, tractor drivers, mechanics, carriers, combine operators and builders, who would park their cars and tractors near the houses. And when three dozen tractors belonging to the owners of one hundred and twenty-eight apartments start immediately at dawn, it may seem to some that the end of the world has come, at that point it will be impossible, by God, to guarantee that some of them will not jump off their balconies in fright.

The first morning of the communist hostel had come. The dawn was bright, one of those that are mentioned in the newspapers. It was a peaceful, quiet, rainbow-clean morning. The sun floated up, with the brightness of a new day, as if it was completely oblivious about the storm brewing in some dormant faraway universe. And this sun carried future events to the unsuspecting residents of the new homes, who were coming to their senses after the housewarming party.

Since these are communist houses, of course, toilets were also included in them. If there is an easily accessible toilet, then there is no person in those buildings who wouldn't want to use it. The proclaimed Shurshit, Temirbek, a resident of the first floor, like all people on this Earth, began a new day with a trip to the toilet. After yesterday's feast, the apartment had not yet been tidied up, half-asleep, stepping over dishes, bags and chests, he grabbed the handle of the restroom, and at that time his feet slapped down into some kind of liquid. As usual, he began to grumble at his wife, believing that she accidentally spilled water on the floor. However, his nose caught a suspicious smell, and he, realizing that this was no ordinary water at all, froze in place. Since he was distracted by the liquid surrounding his legs - he pulled the toilet handle towards himself without much thought, and due to the inertia, as they say, what next happened, happened. The slurry that had accumulated in the toilet rushed over him like a shaft.

He jumped back into the corridor. Temirbek's family woke up from their sleep and immediately found themselves in the noise of this bedlam. Inside the toilet, sewage was pouring out of a thick black pipe with loose fittings, and this eruption had no end. It can be assumed that the inhabitants of the upper apartments indulged in the pleasure of using communal amenities. Temirbek instantly flew up the flight of stairs. And as if reporting an enemy invasion, he pounded his Tatar neighbour's door with his fist. The door was opened by a thin, yellow-faced old woman with glasses.

"Ni kirak sizge*?" She asked.

"Oh god! Lady, Do not touch your toilet. God has cursed us!"

He pushed the old woman aside, bursting into the apartment, shouting:

**Ni kirak sizge – 'what do you need?' in Tatar*

"Who's in the toilet?"

"Oh, God save our souls, what is this about?"

"I won't ask again, who is in the toilet?"

"Ibatullah is in there."

"Everything has gone to hell, Ibatulla!" Temirbek pulled on the handle of the toilet door:

"Ibatulla, come out of here!" He demanded. "Quick!"

Ibatullah's strained voice was heard:

"Give me a moment."

"Forget 'a moment', come out now! My apartment is being carried away by a flood. Don't sit on that toilet. Whether or not you finished the duty or not – get out soon!"

Ibatullah came out, very embarrassed, his face was covered in red spots.

"God, these Kozakhlars* won't even let you sit on the toilet normally," he tried to joke. "Well, what do you need?"

Temirbek quickly explained to him the essence of the matter. Then Ibatullah opened the toilet door once again, and seeing a leaking pipe, yelled at the top of his voice. They both ran to the third floor where an Uzbek, Islamzhan, was living. They explained the situation to him.

---

* *Kozakhlar – another word for Kazakhs.*

"It can't be," he shook his head. "Surely this place can't be breaking down after only one day."

"Hey, your 'surely' and 'can't be' don't really matter if my apartment is already full of sewage. A little more, and all that crap is going to float into your apartment."

The three of them ran to the fourth floor. Where Gamrakeli, a Georgian warehouse manager, was living. He, apparently, had just left the toilet, fastening his belt as the men suddenly appeared.

"Oh, gammarjoba my friends!" He was very happy.

"Oh god, leave your 'gammarjoba' to yourself, just don't go in the toilet anymore!"

"Why?"

"Well, because... this and that..."

Serenity reigned on the fifth floor. The electrician, Ivan Krivonosov, had settled there. After the men clarified the situation to him, he shrugged his shoulders.

"What do you want from me?"

"We'll go to the authorities together. We will write a statement that we did not have time to move to a new house, as our apartments were flooded with sewer water."

"I don't have time today," he said, taking a sip of ice-cold tap water from a cup. "I have to bring my wife from the city, you go yourself. Whosever apartments the water has flooded, let them go and file the report.

A lot of time will pass before it reaches the fifth floor."

"You're being quite inhumane on you part," Temirbek, the proclaimed Shurshit, said earnestly. "I don't care how you lived before, but right now, right here, we live one under the other, we have a common fate, if the neighbour from above does not care about the people below, what will life in this country become? Come and take a look at my apartment and trust me, you'll want to run away to the ends of the earth the moment you'll see it."

They went down to the first floor and entered Temirbek's apartment. His wife and children, pinching their noses, stood there in rubber boots, surrounded by a dam they built from rags and old clothes to protect them from the flowing water, using all their strength to direct the incoming fetid slurry through a threshold into the street. The Georgian, Garmakeli, accidently knocked the door's threshold out of its place, and the collection of everyone's human waste poured out as sludge between the men's feet, having gained strength, it cascaded down along the flight of stairs.

And only then did they notice that the residents of the other entrances were preoccupied with the same problem, which they had been busy dealing with for an hour, immersed in the fight against the dashing water.

After a while, the inhabitants of both buildings rushed out into the yard.

***

The night before, all the authorities of the collected farm gathered at the house of Pashat Barakatov, where it was announced that the report had been sent to the district, after which they stayed up all night and only went to bed in the morning hours. According to an unwritten rule of a special category of leaders, the chairman, the party organizer, the chief agronomist, the manager, all had to sleep on the floor in the main hall. And they, snoring freely, calmly fell into a deep dream. When ten people entered the front room, one after another, covered in God knows what, Pashat's mother, who was spinning threads with her spindle, shouted in fright: "Kitty!" and jumped up.

"Where is that opraulaish?" Temirbek, the proclaimed Shurshit, asked the old woman
calmly.

"Eh... he recently... oh God, Temirbek, is that you? What is the matter with you – oh but there is no face on you, as if the devil is chasing you? Are you healthy?"

"I'm healthy, healthy," Temirbek began to say, trying not to waste time. "The bosses are needed."

"They… have been gone for a long time."

"Where?"

"How do I know; they don't report to me."

"Shit!" Temirbek cursed in exclamation. "Our homes are flooding with water, and they're just dandling around who knows where!"

At this time, the snoring of a friendly male quartet seeped through the tightly closed door of the hall. Having solved the riddle of this snoring, Temirbek and Ibatulla, in spite of the old woman's screeching, opened the door and slipped into the hall. And it seemed to them that they found themselves in a small MTS. It looked like the carcasses of freshly slaughtered cattle were piled up, the men raised such thick snores that the walls trembled, and the ceiling was seconds from floating off into the sky.

Just then, three more men entered the hall, rushing from different sides, they barely woke up and raised the snorers to their feet. The chiefs, shaking their heads, looking at them with dull eyes, as if seeing before them Munkir and Nankir, the angels of death demanding an answer, could not understand anything. Then, somehow understanding the essence of the matter, they muttered: "Okay, go, we'll be right there," and as soon as the people left the hall, they again fell on their beds.

When the chiefs, clutching their heads every now and then due to the fogginess and noise – found themselves near the seven-story buildings, it was already noon, and the people, losing patience, were seething with anger. At that point, the first test had begun.

"You are all ignoramuses!" Pashat said after listening to the irritated people. "You are wild people and are not accustomed to living in the city. Barely having moved in, you already slaughtered many sheep, started cleaning your offal in the toilet bowl, and flushed all your garbage down the very same toilet. For violating the rules of the communist hostel, I should be fining you all right now."

"Is that really how they do things in the city? Having barely moved in, we now have to pay fines?" Old Meldesh shouted from his balcony, squinting his eyes. "Do you think we're a bunch of idiots? First and foremost, you need to be held accountable for all of this."

Suddenly he leaned out over the railing and looked up where he could see the head of a girl leaning over the railing of her balcony on the fifth floor, he shouted to her:

"Hey! Tell your stupid father not to go to the toilet, and not to flush. Are you all deaf up there or something, even if we tried to hit your door with an axe, you probably wouldn't open it, would you?" The girl silently slipped into the apartment.

After a long noisy trial, they went around all the apartments. Everything turned out to be true. They decided to invite a commissioner over from the district. Prior to the arrival of the commission, they agreed not to flush the toilet, not to use the bath, not to open the taps in the kitchen.

The commissioner arrived a week later. She didn't stay long. She made her conclusions right away. It turns out that the 'Socialism' department made a sensational discovery in the world of multi-storey building construction: It never occurred to the collective farmers to lay underground sewers and connect them to high-rise buildings in order to eliminate the difference between the city and the aul.

"That's the problem, you know, I kept thinking, 'How did they build everything in just five months!' Now I know…" After listening to the commissioner, the chairman of the collective farm looked menacingly at Pashat and Sepentai. As if to say, "Well, get ready for jail, there is no other way out."

"Well, if we're going to jail, at least we're all going," Pashat said plaintively, as if finding at least some consolation in these words.

This exceptional event also reached the local region. Meetings, party bureaus, severe reprimands were held and made. However, reprimands won't fix a building, they can't build a sewer. After long meetings, the district authorities came to the unanimous opinion that it was necessary to start work on sewerage. Overnight, the best equipment in the region was brought to the 'Socialism' department in order to start work the next day, before news of this disaster spread all over the world.

A large pit was dug a few kilometres from the village, and a trench half a meter deep was dug away from it, extending all the way to the high-rise buildings of Socialism.

At this time, the population of both buildings lived like hell. Some returned to their old huts, others, subject to strict discipline, cooked food in the yard on the hearths and relieved themselves in the steppe, and only came home to spend the night.

The grandson of the old man Meldesh was supposed to marry, they were only waiting for a housewarming party, and soon his wedding came up. They asked him to wait, but the grandson insisted on his own. When they were preparing for the wedding, the mother-in-law of Zhaparkhan, the old man's neighbour, had unfortunately died. And this family met its first mourning in the new home. In this regard, the residents of the building faced a particularly shocking situation: relatives who came to the funeral began shouting: "Bauyrym*!" But some accidently entered the apartment where a great feast was flaring up to celebrate the marriage, and the guests who arrived for the wedding ended up in the apartment where people were wailing a mourning cry with might and main. After that, people became accustomed to this unconstrained life, the villagers began to avoid each other, quarrels and scandals broke out more and more often, little by little people stopped communicating.

At first, the sewers were being dug with enthusiasm, but gradually the work subsided. Two and a half months later, a pipe was laid out, and the ground under the skyscrapers began to dry out. Either engineering calculations turned out to be inaccurate, or the ground under the houses was loose, be that as it may, with the drying of the soil, both buildings began to sink into the ground, noticeably tilting towards each other.

The authorities urgently stopped work and ordered the residents of the buildings to be evicted. It was necessary for some people to put up tents and temporarily move into them, as they had managed

**Bauyrym - a ritual cry in the funeral customs of the Kazakhs.*

to destroy their unsightly old houses in the joy of the housewarming event.

And again, there was shouting and screaming, the people who were accustomed to living in the buildings were indignant. The district authorities again gathered for a meeting to decide: What should they do? During the hot harvest season, the people were not willing to work, everyone thought only about themselves and their homes, about their unfortunate situation.

1986

BONAPARTE'S WEDDING

A COMEDY

DULAT ISSABEKOV "THE CONFRONTATION"

CHARACTERS:

BONAPARTE
AUGANBEK
ISPANALI
ABDASHIM
ULTUGAN
AKSAKAL RAT *[An aksakal is the name given in Kazakhstan to a male elder, traditionally the leader of the village]*
CHAPAI
ROLLAN
TASBOLAT
KASHPIROVSKY

Cheerful music.

A young boy is running around the stage. The boy is Chapai – Bonaparte's younger brother.

– Hurrah! It's decided! In a month Bonaparte will bring a bride into the house!

Everyone is invited to the wedding! Come along! Share our joy with us! There will be a huge celebration in our house next month! Come along! Come along!

The cheerful music and dancing continues.

***

From two sides of the stage, people of various ages walk into the centre, looking worried. They come together, whisper about something, then quickly separate.

Some of the remarks can be heard above the concerned whispers. The women place their hands over their faces, clearly appalled by something shameful.

There is a general commotion.

What a disgrace! How are we going to look people in the eye now? How awful!

The real shame is still to come! If their parents find out about this travesty then there will be hell to pay!

I'd rather die than walk around with such shame!

We will never hear the end of this, as long as we are alive!

Why did this have to happen to us! What a disgrace! It's awful!

Oh my, what are their parents going to say when they find out about this?

Now we've got the stench of this scandal on us, do we at least have the right to have our say about it? Can't we object?

Oh my-my! There will be nothing left, we'll all be thrown to the wolves!

*** *The same boy is running again.*

Bonaparte is getting married! The wedding is in a month! Everyone is invited! Come along! Share our joy with us!

ISPANALI. What is your name, boy?

CHAPAI. Chapai.

ISPANALI. And are you really preparing for a wedding?

CHAPAI. Yes! I have already written you an invitation.

AUGANBEK. Oh have you indeed? And have you written one for me as well?

CHAPAI. No, I haven't got round to yours yet. Here's your invitation…

(Chapai gives the invitation to Ispanali).

ISPANALI. Is your father at home?

CHAPAI. He was there when I left.

AUGANBEK. In that case run home as fast as you can. Make sure your father and mother don’t go anywhere. We will come to see them in a while. There is something urgent to discuss.

CHAPAI. Uncle Ispanali, uncle Auganbek, are you upset about something?

Are you both alright?

ISPANALI. We will tell you when we get there. Now run home...

CHAPAI. I still have a lot of invitations to –...

AUGANBEK. *(Interrupting).* When someone tells you to run, you run. You’re too smart for your own good. You’ll still have time to hand out your invitations. That’s if there will be a wedding to invite anyone to! *(The boy runs away).*

***

Bonaparte's home. In the house are his father Abdashim, his mother Ultugan, Auganbek, Ispanali and the village aksakal Rat. This is the village's 'emergency committee', which gathers whenever there is an extraordinary event. Everyone is looking very serious, sitting with crossed arms and furrowed brows.

RAT. Well everyone, let's begin. Where are those two idiots? Call them here!

Abdashim enters with Ultugan. They walk gloomily, with their heads bowed guiltily.

Eh, you, you pair of sinners! Is it true that your offspring, who is planning to get married in a month, was never circumcised?

ABDASHIM. Well... um... you see....

RAT. I'll ask you again: is it true or is it not true that he wasn't circumcised? Speak, don't be embarrassed...

ABDASHIM. If that's what people are saying then it must be true. How should we know, how can we check, do you expect us to inspect him?

RAT. Oh, you odious cretin! Did you hear what he's suggesting?

Apostate!

ISPANALI. Eh, Abdashim! If you don't know which of your six sons are circumcised and which aren't, evil spirits must have come over you, wouldn't you say?

ABDASHIM. It was all just a blur… I had too much work, there was no time... It slipped my mind...

AUGANBEK. You're not the only one who has work to think about. None of us are free from it either...

ISPANALI. And our aksakal, Rat, has eleven sons and nineteen grandsons – and he didn't forget about any of them. Isn't that right, aksakal?

RAT. Heaven forbid I could ever be so careless!

ISPANALI. Does this infidel think that the six sons that God gave him are a burden on him? And aksakal Rat, isn't he the one who once upon a time raised six hundred sheep on the kolkhoz *[Soviet collective farm]*, and knew each of them like the back of his hand? He knew which of the ewes were pregnant and which weren't. Isn't that right, aksakal?

RAT. Yes, of course! Of course!

ISPANALI. Did you hear that? Six hundred sheep! And you've only got six sons and still can't keep track of them!

ABDASHIM. Yes, but those were sheep. A person isn't an animal…

AUGANBEK. Yes, exactly: a person isn't an animal. But the two of you are! ULTUGAN. Me as well?

AUGANBEK. Yes, both of you. I don't see any justification for your behaviour.

ULTUGAN. My dear aunt and uncle, don't you remember the day I received a gold medal from the president himself? And don't you remember the time when we were all gathered around the dastarkhan *[a dining table laid out for a special occasion]*, and you praised us in front of the guests? Oh, my precious relatives, what has changed since then?

AUGANBEK. *(A little slower).* Hmm... yes, perhaps I did give you some praise.

But opinions of people can always change. And how can I not change my mind, after hearing such shameful news?

ISPANALI. Well, well! Instead of admitting their mistakes, these idiots are putting all the blame on us!

AUGANBEK. Exactly! And after abandoning your children to the whims of fate, what have you been doing ever since?

ABDASHIM. Why do you say we abandoned them? No one abandoned them – they didn't raise themselves...

ISPANALI. You know what you can do with your "raising"! No, how on earth did you manage to forget that one of your children hadn't been circumcised? It'd be better if you told us that!

ABDASHIM. As you know, just as our children were starting to grow up, Perestroika began...

ISPANALI. And did you do anything worthwhile before Perestroika?

ABDASHIM. Before Perestroika we had atheism. You said yourself that circumcision was a thing of the past. You went after the mullahs who still performed them. It even got to a point where boys who had been snipped weren't allowed in the Komsomol [*Communist youth organisation]*. Aksakal Rat, give us your sacred word: isn't it true that it was forbidden?

RAT. Eh, is it really worth digging up the past? They did all sorts of filthy things to us – Heaven forbid we have to go through it again!

ISPANALI. But it is your fault that you so dutifully followed every order from above. The authorities gave us orders, and we gave you orders. You should have followed your grandfathers' ways, and not blindly listened to orders that did so much harm to our nation!

AUGANBEK. Exactly! Muslims whose faith was strong didn't let anyone push them off the righteous path, even when they were threatened with the sharp spear of atheism. Even the secretary of the district committee, Esentai, brought all three of his children to aksakal Rat one night, under cover of darkness. And why? To have them circumcised. Isn't that right, aksakal?

RAT. Eh… well... sometimes ... it is the work of God…

ULTUGAN. They say that when Esentai himself was a small boy, it was our respected aksakal who made a Muslim of him....

ISPANALI. Stop it! It isn't good to spread dirty rumours.

AUGANBEK. *(Laughing)*. Oh, my poor uncle! Is there anyone in this village you haven't seen? Even the secretary of the district committee...

ISPANALI. Stop your chattering! Abdashim, where is your infidel son?

RAT. Careful! You mustn't call a Muslim an infidel!

ISPANALI. And what must we call a man who wasn't circumcised? Call your son here – we'll see what he has to say for himself.

VOICES. Call Bonaparte! Get Bonaparte here!

ISPANALI. Bonaparte! And anyway, how could you give that scatterbrain son of yours such a ridiculous name? Couldn't you think of anything more suitable?

ULTUGAN. Oh my dear uncle, wasn't it you who gave him that name, when we were all welcoming him into the world? You know, there is a country called France, and they, like us, have a lot of brave men. If you go there you'll see that there are lots of surnames like Conrad, Naimann, Aragon. If the French, out of respect for us, can use Kazakh names for their surnames, then why can't we name our children after their nation's heroes? Wasn't it you who used to shout that "We mustn't let our horizons be narrowed by nationalism"?

ISPANALI. That was the policy of the time! My father and mother also gave me a regal name: Ispanali! And that one they named Auganbek.

ULTUGAN. You called my third baby Ho Chi Minh! By the time we applied for a passport for him, we only just managed to convince them to change it to the Kazakh 'Koishiman'. These days there are all sorts of half-forgotten leaders and relics from past eras.

Chapai, Shchors! And where is Bonaparte?

VOICES: He's coming, he's coming!

A tall, gangly man enters the house. Here it isn't by any means necessary to describe him in great detail. This can be left to the director, and depends on the resources that the theatre has. Themost important thing is that the character has an air of comedy about him.

AUGANBEK. In front of you stands His Excellence, Bonaparte, son of Abdashim!

ISPANALI. Listen here boy, why don't you hurry when people call for you? And where have you been, you have caused these good people all sorts of pains...

BONAPARTE. We are strengthening the material and technical basis for communism.

VOICES. What did he say? What is that nincompoop talking about?

BONAPARTE. I said I have been busy at work.

AUGANBEK. Ah, then why didn't you say so! If the material and technical basis for communism depends on the work you do, then there is no hope for it! And what do you do there?

BONAPARTE. Roosevelt's car got stuck in a ditch, and Churchill and I are trying to haul it out with a tractor.

AUGANBEK. Oh you idiot, are you in your right

mind?

BONAPARTE. Well, it was you who raised me…

Bektur enters with a newspaper in his hands. Without paying attention to anyone, his eyes still glued to the newspaper, he walks straight through the group, dividing them into two parts.

BEKTUR. Roosevelt! Churchill! Bonaparte! Chapai! Shchors! Kazakh simpletons, you can't even name your children properly! Ispanali! Iranbek! Irakbek! Hahaha!

He leaves.

ISPANALI. Where did that odd man come from?

AUGANBEK. Who invited him? Why did he come, why did he leave?

ABDASHIM. Don't you know who that was? Wasn't that Bektur, the village poet?

ULTUGAN. That poor young man... He used to work on building sites. He became a pretty good bricklayer, until last year when a brick landed on his head. The poor lad, since then he's been a poet. He walks around just like that…

ISPANALI. Let's not get distracted. Bonaparte, Your Excellency, how are you feeling, are you ready to take a wife?

BONAPARTE. I am!

AUGANBEK. My foot he's ready!

BONAPARTE. And what do you need to be ready? I'm in healthy mind, all my organs work, and you've already given the girl's family half of the dowry. I've seen the girl herself twice. I like her. And she doesn't mind being friends with me either. What else do you need?

ISPANALI. Just listen to what comes out of his mouth! What else do you need?

I'll tell you what else you need!

BONAPARTE. What?

ISPANALI. What, he's asking! Eh, Auganbek, tell that moron what else you need to take a wife... You don't have any shame – you've never had any!

AUGANBEK. Why are we tiptoeing around the issue? Why don't we just cut to the chase? All your relatives are making plans for your wedding, and you haven't even been circumcised. Is this true?

BONAPARTE. Well how should I know?

ISPANALI. Oh, you...! And who do you think is going to know, if not you? Me?

BONAPARTE. Well, my parents...

AUGANBEK. *Eurgh!* Are you hearing this nonsense? His parents! Your parents don't have a clue about anything. Their brains went soft years ago!

ABDASHIM. Eh, Auganbek! Do you think you can just say out loud anything that comes into your head? It's as if you think you're so clever, and we're stupid!

AUGANBEK. Then why aren't you managing your son better?! What else do you expect us to say about this?

ULTUGAN. Listen, uncle! Seeing as our aksakal is present, I wanted to do the polite thing and stay silent. But you're taking us for some kind of dunces – not letting us speak a word of our own, and treating us like imbeciles. I, praise God, brought six sons and three daughters into this world. And at each of our meetings, you and your activist wife order people to "support the wish of the president to bring the number of Kazakhs to twenty million". You may be giving the orders, but it's us who are giving birth! If we're losing our minds then there is a reason for it. While you are spending all your time fighting to get heating into our homes, we don't want to be there with only one child.

ISPANALI. Well said, auntie, that's shown him! *(To Auganbek).* She is talking about you too, beaurocrat! Maybe now you might stop blowing hot air and start actually doing something. Haha!

RAT. Stop this idle chatter! We have an issue to discuss!

AUGANBEK. Then let's get to the issue. So it appears you don't know yourself whether you have been circumcised or not? You really are a simpleton! It doesn't take a genius to work it out…

ISPANALI. Eh, Auganbek! What are we doing getting cross at each other like this? Can't he just go outside, take a look and come back?

AUGANBEK. But of course! Why didn't we think of this sooner? Bonaparte! Get up and come with me! We're going to go and see something!

Auganbek and Ispanali clumsily drag Bonaparte out.

CHAPAI. Dad, Mum, is Bonaparte not going to get married?

ABDASHIM. Just wait a little, son. It all depends on what your uncles decide when they come back.

CHAPAI. Aksakal Rat, please let Bonaparte have his wedding. I have already given invitations to half of the village. What will we tell them?

RAT. Patience, my boy, patience…

CHAPAI. I have seen Bonaparte's bride. She's such a pretty girl! There was a beauty contest and she was named Miss District...

ABDASHIM. Then we're in big trouble…

CHAPAI. Why?

ABDASHIM. Because if a girl who they called Miss District hears about this, we'll be the laughing stock of the whole region.

ULTUGAN. Do you think this backstreet beauty queen was brought to us on gilded lilies? I saw her last year at a gathering somewhere. There's nothing special about her – she's an ordinary Kazakh girl, with dark skin and a flat nose. There's a rumour going around that her father spent most of his savings to buy her that title.

CHAPAI. That's not true! People only say that because they're jealous. She's actually a very beautiful girl!

ULTUGAN. So what if she's pretty? My son is handsome as well...

Auganbek and Ispanali enter.

AUGANBEK. We have our answer...

ISPANALI. He definitely hasn't been circumcised.

RAT. And where is he now?

AUGANBEK. He's gone back to work. As he was leaving, he said that if he didn't get that girl he would hang himself.

ABDASHIM. What? Why was he talking about hanging himself?

ULTUGAN. Because of his bride? To hell with her! No bride will ever be worthy of my little boy!

Ultugan runs away, her head in her hands.

ISPANALI. But no-one knew anything about this matter until today! Why did they have to make a problem out of it? And why today, of all days?

ABDASHIM. What problem?

ISPANALI. What problem? It's like you're mentally ill! We've been talking about the problem all day. The problem is with your son's unblessed appendage.

AUGANBEK. Look, everything had been happily forgotten. So why bring this unpleasantness up again?

ABDASHIM. Wasn't it you who began this conversation yourselves? Where were you earlier? And you think of yourselves as close relatives! Where is your empathy? You're not even trying to cover up this mess, you want to discuss it further... Anything to create more gossip...

ISPANALI. Here he goes again, the infidel! If I were you I wouldn't make any accusations myself. Instead of admitting that it's his fault and keeping quiet, he's trying to stick his claws into us... He could at least look embarrassed. Even aksakal Rat is embarrassed...

ABDASHIM. The aksakal is at fault too – if he is the eldest among us, shouldn't he have enlightened us? At least remind us?

AUGANBEK. Of course!

ISPANALI. So what is this, you are getting us out of the way so that you can disrespect the aksakal? Shut your mouth you infidel!

ABDASHIM. I can't be an infidel – I have never once broken the laws of Sharia.

ISPANALI. You say you have never broken the laws? Then why don't you know how to read the Koran? Hasn't fifty years been enough?

ABDASHIM. Oh yes, and of course you're the perfect Muslim! You don't even wash your feet before you enter the mosque.

ISPANALI. Sometimes I do, sometimes I don't… Who are you to decide how clean I am? Do you also check whether I take a bucket of water into the latrine? Then you really are an infidel – bringing shame on yourself by not showing your son the righteous path!

AUGANBEK. Eh! What's the matter with you? Your face has already turned red from so much yelling! And for what? Stop this senseless quarrel!

ABDASHIM. I didn't start this quarrel, you did! You called me an imbecile, you said I was mentally ill. You called me an infidel!

ISPANALI. You don't read namaz *[Islamic prayers]*, you didn't get your son circumcised, you eat sausage, you drink vodka – who are you if not an infidel?

ABDASHIM. Eh, Ispanali! You're an expert at harassing people, too direct, even when a person doesn't want you to be... And here you are with your "infidel"! You know that her family lives on the other side of the railway tracks, with dozens of Russian families. They have nothing to do with circumcisions and namaz. But they also want to go to heaven. And they have such adorable children. And their girls are so beautiful...

At this moment aksakal Rat, who until then had been sitting in silence, joins the argument.

RAT. Imbeciles! What on earth do you think you are doing with all your senseless chattering? Did anyone ask you who goes to heaven and who goes to hell, who is beautiful and who is a shaitan [evil spirit]?

ABDASHIM. And if no-one asks, does that mean we can't say? How can we not be angry at those who called themselves atheists when they were working on the kolkhoz, then became mullahs as soon as the Party was gone? It's not for nothing that we have the saying "Sufis are devils who had nothing else to do".

RAT. That's already more than enough idle chatter. What do you think we should do now?

Silence.

ISPANALI. It's only a month until the bride arrives, what can we do? He's been walking around like this until now, so let him stay like this. Do you think someone is going to be spying on him? Atheism has to leave a trace of kindness too.

RAT. Stop joking around and get to the point!

AUGANBEK. Fine, I will get to the point: Bonaparte must be circumcised straight away. Today, at the very latest! This is the most correct decision to take.

ABDASHIM. Today? Oh my, and what if the boy doesn't agree to it?

AUGANBEK. He will agree to it. You will make him agree to it.

ABDASHIM. Oh my, but he isn't a small child – you can't just stroke his hair and tell him it isn't going to hurt. He's a grown jigit *[horseman]*! What if he grabs the knife out of the mullah's hands and stabs someone?

AUGANBEK. Then your job is to tie his hands and legs before you bring him to the mullah.

ABDASHIM. There is only a month until the wedding… What if he hasn't healed by then, what will we do?

AUGANBEK. Why wouldn't he heal – is someone going to put a curse on him? We had to go through this once as well, you know. It took a couple of days – three at most.

ABDASHIM. Once… We were young then...

ISPANALI. Why are we wasting our breath talking about this? What if it takes ten days, or fifteen? If you chopped his hand off it wouldn't take fifteen days to heal.

Auganbek, who had been sitting for a while lost in his own thoughts, smiling and rubbing his knee, suddenly gives a loud guffaw.

RAT. Have you lost your mind? What's wrong with you?!

AUGANBEK. We will never live this down...

RAT. With who?

AUGANBEK. With the bride. It'll be fine if he heals in time. But if he doesn't…

RAT. Enough of your stupid jokes! Unless you want to bring shame upon your family, let us get to work, starting today. Set up a yurt in the yard outside your home – we will make that son of yours presentable before lunchtime.

EVERYONE. – Yes!
We will do everything as you say.
Come on Abdashim, call your son…

ABDASHIM. I'm just thinking, will they let him leave his work?

ISPANALI. What, is he such a brilliant worker that they can't do without him for an afternoon? We can lift his car out of a ditch ourselves.

ABDASHIM. Then let's go…

Bektur appears again, with a newspaper in his hands.

BEKTUR. In accordance with the decision of a three-day meeting, and in order to obtain a detailed answer to the question "What needs to be done to facilitate the growth and prosperity of the village?" our representative Tasbolat, to whom we have all given money, has gone to Austria for personal talks with a soothsayer called Globa.

Bektur leaves again, but no-one pays much attention to him. They all look confused.

AUGANBEK. That poor man must have taken a real blow to the head...

ISPANALI. I don't think he was ever circumcised either.

Ultugan runs in, panting for breath.

ULTUGAN. My boy is nowhere to be seen! Someone saw him running towards the river, screaming "I'd rather drown than bring such shame upon myself!"

ISPANALI. Who saw him?

ULTUGAN. Churchill.

ISPANALI. Oh for goodness' sake! Come on, Auganbek! We need to find Bonaparte quickly and bring him here. And you, Abdashim, put up the yurt in the middle of the yard. Aksakal Rat, you can start sharpening your knife.

RAT. My knife is always ready.

ISPANALI. Listen, everyone! No-one apart from us can find out that Bonaparte is being circumcised.

ULTUGAN. So what can we tell the men he works with? They might ask...

ISPANALI. Tell them that he has fallen ill.

ABDASHIM. With what?

AUGANBEK. Does it matter? There are a lot of diseases to choose from. Say he has AIDS, or bird flu – just make sure no-one else sticks their nose in around here.

ABDASHIM. Bite that tongue of yours, Auganbek! You should be ashamed of yourself...

AUGANBEK. Eh, Abdashim, you could be a little more careful yourself. You have made your bed, now lie in it.

ABDASHIM. Insolence! You scoundrel! So now you have decided to mock me, have you? (*Abdashim throws himself at Auganbek)*

Auganbek and Ispanali laugh and run away.

***

Inside the yurt. Bonaparte is lying on a bed. Auganbek and Ispanali enter.

AUGANBEK. How are you feeling?

Bonaparte is silent.

AUGANBEK. I asked you how you are feeling – answer me!

Bonaparte merely gulps.

ISPANALI. How are you feeling, you worthless dog?

BONAPARTE. I'm lying down, as you can see...

AUGANBEK. Yes, we can see that you are lying down. How are you feeling?

BONAPARTE. How could I be feeling? I'm lying down.

ISPANALI. Well, um... Do you feel any better?

BONAPARTE. I don't think so...

AUGANBEK. Eh, you have been in bed for two weeks now! Why aren't you feeling better?

BONAPARTE. What do you want me to say?

ISPANALI. I don't think this waste of space even wants to get better. There are only two weeks until his bride arrives, and here he is in bed, without a care in the world!

AUGANBEK. It's no use just lying around, you need to try to get better.

BONAPARTE. How do I try to get better?

ISPANALI. Work it out for yourself! Or summon the spirits of your forefathers.

BONAPARTE. I already am summoning them.

AUGANBEK. Then do it better – you have to really want to.

BONAPARTE. Should I be involving my forefathers in such a shameful matter?

ISPANALI. Listen, I think he has a point here...

AUGANBEK. Or more likely he is just being cunning, and has found a way to lay around at home instead of going to work. It can't be taking so long to heal. It just isn't possible.

ISPANALI. You're right. His bed is made for him, the house is nice and cool, he has his meals brought to him on a tray… Let's have a look ourselves to see how he is healing…

AUGANBEK. How?

ISPANALI. Can you really not guess? Here, lift his blanket up. I'll take a look myself.

Auganbek takes the white blanket away from Bonaparte and lifts it up. Ispanali goes around it to look at what is underneath. Ultugan enters.

ULTUGAN. Oh my, what are you doing?

ISPANALI. Will you look at this scoundrel? The wound hasn't even closed! If he was one of us he would already be up and walking around – he must get his skin from his mother's genes.

ULTUGAN. Eh, and what do you have against his mother's genes? If he had taken after his mother he would be galloping like a stallion in three days. My dear Kazakhs, when are you going to stop blaming others for your own shortcomings?

ISPANALI *(Taken by surprise)* Oh, Auntie, when did you get here?

ULTUGAN. Does what you have to say about me depend on where I am? Praise God, his mother's genes are completely pure. Isn't that right? And rumour has it that once upon a time you also took more than two weeks to heal, so if you want to find defects, start by looking at yourself. All of our forefathers were mighty horsemen. One distant ancestor, Borykbai, suffered an injured arm in a battle and chopped it off himself, before killing about a hundred Jungar warriors.

BONAPARTE. Cool! You know, the Jungars had us under their yoke for two hundred years, but two of our ancestors managed to kill about three hundred of them...

AUGANBEK. Will you just listen to this helpless idiot? It's because of his stupid character that he has taken so long to heal.

BONAPARTE. What has my stupid character got to do with anything? I just wanted to ask you for a little less bragging, and a little more truth.

ISPANALI. Don't trouble your little head with the truth. First of all you need to think about getting better.

BONAPARTE. Thinking is no use...

ISPANALI. Well seeing as there is no use, you can get the hell out of here, can't you? If your bride finds out that you are here laying about, then she will probably die of shame.

BONAPARTE. So what are you telling me to do? I would rather have tied a rock to my neck and jumped in the river than go through all this shameful business – but you chased me on your horses, tied me up and dragged me to this bed. This is what happens when you force people to do things that they don't really want to do!

ISPANALI. It seems we have an audience with a philosopher! It would take a year to treat you of all of your ills, Bonaparte, my poor Frenchman!

ULTUGAN. Eh, you are going to exhaust my son with all of your chattering.

Ispanali suddenly laughs loudly.

ISPANALI. Just imagine if some real Frenchmen came here and saw a man called Bonaparte lying in such a state, in a little Kazakh village called Engels! Ha-ha-ha!

Voices in unison:

VOICES: – Everyone to the village club!

We're going to select the village akim [*head of local government*]!

Make sure everyone comes!

Our future is in your hands!

Everyone has to vote!

AUGANBEK. We chose an akim six months ago. What has happened there since?

ISPANALI. There are six parties working in our village. We are always holding meetings here for one of them or the other. Each party is trying to get its representative into power.

ULTUGAN. But none of these representatives ever settle in the village. The akim has changed six times in five years! People are confused, everything is in disarray.

AUGANBEK. The akims are to blame themselves. When they walk among us, like ordinary people, they have some clout – but as soon as they disappear, it's as if the previous akim was still in place.

ISPANALI. It's all because of democracy. As soon as that disaster happened to us, people just calmly stopped going to work.

BONAPARTE. Democracy is just a temporary mishap. The hurricane will run out of steam, and we'll all return to how things were.

ISPANALI. Oh really? Two weeks in bed reading newspapers and I see you've turned into an eminent politician. Listen, if lying around is doing you so much good then maybe you'd better stay here for another month! Or two… Or lay around for three months, then you can establish the Bonaparte Party and put yourself forward to be elected as akim. And if you'll be trying to become an akim, you won't need to get married…

ULTUGAN. As the saying goes, "It isn't the rider who notices the saddle chafing, but the horse – and it isn't a family that notices a worthy man, but the passer-by". Why are you all opening your mouths, if all that comes out is attacks and insults? Why not some kind words to lift the soul? Do you really think that my son is worse than anyone else? When he grows up he will show you what he is really made of. (*Ultugan strokes Bonaparte's head*).

AUGANBEK. Yes, Auntie, you are speaking God's truth. Bonaparte is still just a child. The poor boy has only just been circumcised...*(Auganbek tries to conceal his laughter).*

ULTUGAN. Laugh if you want to. But I'm warning you – he will show all of you. Our family has raised five sergeant majors, two judges, and one high sultan.

AUGANBEK. If you are from such a prestigious family, why did you marry our uncle Abdashim?

ULTUGAN. When the Soviets were in power no Kazakhs were registered as regal sons and daughters – we and our ancestors were cast as down-and-outs, no matter where we came from. But look at us today – none of us have poor roots: all of our ancestors were wealthy landowners, army men, horsemen, khans...

AUGANBEK. So Auntie, are you one of them?

ISPANALI. Listen, are we going to this meeting or not?

AUGANBEK. We can't miss it! If we do then those activists will just push another thief into power. But where has our uncle Abdashim got to?

ULTUGAN. He left to go to the club a long time ago.

ISPANALI. But of course – he has to have his say at every meeting. He was so occupied with them that he forgot to have his son circumcised. (To Bonaparte). While we're gone, try not to fill your head with too many newspapers. Try summoning your mother's ancestors instead. Surely five sergeant majors, two judges and one high sultan will be able to help you?

ULTUGAN. You awful men, wagging your tongues instead of saying something nice!

Ultugan throws the chair she had been sitting on at Ispanali and Auganbek. They both run out of the room.

***

All members of the 'emergency committee' are in the house: the aksakal Rat, Abdashim, Ultugan, Ispanali and Auganbek.
There may be other people present, but we don't need to name them.

ISPANALI. The situation is becoming more complicated, aksakal. There are only ten days until the relatives are introduced, and Bonaparte is still a long way from being healed.

RAT. Have you done everything I told you to do?

ABDASHIM. Everything, aksakal. The imam from the mouse came three times to read namaz. A young mullah also read from the Koran. For five days in a row a shaman blew the smoke from a white chicken onto him. We cut up a black ram, and gave the meat out to poor families. One night we took him to sleep next to the grave of a sacred pilgrim. Three times after midnight we shot our weapons outside the house. To make sure that there was always food on the table, we ate almost all of the food that we had bought for the wedding.

ULTUGAN. Are mullahs these days turning into

businessmen? Don't take another step towards the patient…

Aksakal Rat gives Ultugan a disapproving glance.

ABDASHIM. Look, everyone – the words of our aksakal are the most important. People have only ever accepted his advice with words of gratitude.

AUGANBEK. I suppose it couldn't hurt to take him to the doctor?

ULTUGAN. Does this village have even one slightly competent doctor? The hospital went to pieces a long time ago. The only person there now is a young lad, and he doesn't know his arse from his elbow.

AUGANBEK. They say he isn't even a doctor. When he gives you an injection the needle goes all the way through your arm and out the other side.

ISPANALI. He was hired by activists from the "Tauekel" party at the last meeting!

AUGANBEK. But the party "Praise to God" is on their case – if their candidate becomes the village's akim then he will be straight over to the hospital. It's promises that win elections!

ULTUGAN. To hell with all of them! While they're

trying to become akims you get headaches from their promises. People are tired of these scoundrels.

ABDASHIM. You know, I went to see that doctor the other day. He barked at me: "Whoever did your son's circumcision, get him to treat it. If you had asked me to do it he would be fine by now. It's your ignorance that has done all this!" Then he threw me out!

AUGANBEK. He's a wise man...

Auganbek gives a hearty laugh. Ispanali joins in. Abdashim and Ultugan follow suit.

RAT. This is not a time to be laughing! Eh, you, layabouts and bickerers, laughing about matters like these is sinful!

ISPANALI. Aksakal, don't be so harsh – they say that laughing at silly pieces of gossip lightens the soul. Ever since that man-child has been circumcised, we, his relatives, have taken on all of his work.

Abdashim is also doing everything that he can. Kydy-ata is always unhappy with us about something, but the treatments we have tried on Bonaparte haven't had any effect. Our failures are due to ecology – I think it's because the air is polluted!

RAT. It's your conscience that is polluted. Your

conscience!

ABDASHIM. I don't remember ever wishing anyone ill, or doing anything even a tiny bit malicious. So I don't understand why we are being subjected to all this abuse.

RAT. It isn't only you. Everyone sitting here is to blame. Everyone – the whole village! The whole district! If all that you have said is a lie; if you read the Koran over a dastarkhan, where bad water and bad food are placed together; if such words as sin and beneficence are completely forgotten; if so many ignorant mullahs have appeared... then how can the whole planet not be overtaken by evil and sabotage? Punishment! Punishment! This too is punishment! This is the answer God has sent down to us!

Rat leaves, without looking at anyone.
Everyone is silent.

ISPANALI. So what are we going to do?

AUGANBEK. What do you mean?

ISPANALI. There are only ten days until we have to receive the bride. So what are we going to do?

AUGANBEK. Within ten days that charlatan will be able to drive there and back!

ISPANALI. And if he can't?

AUGANBEK. Then… Then you will be the groom and you'll drive there instead.

ISPANALI. What?! Have you lost your mind? How can I be the groom?

AUGANBEK. Easy! We will give you a wash and a shave, and dress you up.

ISPANALI. And if they realise that they are being deceived?

AUGANBEK. They won't. We will leave at night, and come back at night too. Luckily the electricity in their village has gone off. Someone stole their cable.

ISPANALI. Are you being serious? The bride's friends and aunts will want to go through the groom's pockets, and lay a meal out for him. We aren't going to be sitting in the dark not able to see each other.

AUGANBEK. Then don't look at anyone, keep your head down. Don't talk, and don't laugh too loudly. All you have to do is smile.

ISPANALI. So you want everyone to think there is something wrong with the groom? Then you can go yourself. You're three years younger than me. And you look more like Bonaparte than I do.

AUGANBEK. No, no, I can't!

ISPANALI. Why not?

AUGANBEK. Because one of my wives is from

that village. And the other one has relatives there. They will recognise me there straight away!

ISPANALI. Of all the villages in Kazakhstan to get your wives from...

AUGANBEK. You talk as if he only looked in one village...

ISPANALI. And it's still giving us headaches...

Our old friend Bektur enters.
As before his head is buried in a newspaper.
He reads aloud and pays no attention to anyone.

BEKTUR. The Chinese government, just 70-80 kilometres from the border with Kazakhstan, conducted a second test of a 55-kiloton nuclear weapon at the Lobnor test site. The Kazakh government and the Semey-Nevada movement did not issue any warning to the Chinese authorities!

Bektur leaves.

AUGANBEK *(Glancing at Bektur)*. Eh, we have enough to worry about as it is, we don't need another problem. Get out of here!

ISPANALI. That poor man really needs to be seriously treated. As soon as we have Bonaparte's wedding out of the way, we'll turn our attention to that poor moron.

AUGANBEK. Well, what do you suggest? Are you going to be a groom for the day, or have you got a better idea?

ISPANALI. Ten years ago my distant cousin Tazakulu had a bride brought home to him. That day he had got drunk, and ended up sleeping it off in a police cell, so I took her into the house instead of him. So what now, do you want me to do the same again?

AUGANBEK. Well, since you have some experience...

ISPANALI. So am I the replacement groom for everyone in this village? No, no-one is going to believe me again, I'm not doing it!

AUGANBEK. Eh, let's have another look at Bonaparte. It's just impossible that he still can't get up.

ISPANALI. Let's give the patient some peace.

***

Inside the yurt. Bonaparte is on the bed, reading a newspaper. Auganbek and Ispanali enter.

ISPANALI. So, pea-brain, any change?

Bonaparte doesn't reply.

AUGANBEK. He doesn't even look at us. He could at least have said hello.

Silence.

ISPANALI. If this week you can't get your useless body out of bed, Your Imperial Highness, then one of us will go and fetch your bride. What do you think of that, Your Highness?

More silence.

AUGANBEK. Just look at this pea-brain, lying around without a care in the world! And making us do all his work for him! I think his bed rest has turned him into a real sloth. But it's no surprise: his relatives on his mother's side were lazy as well.

Ultugan enters. She hears what Auganbek says.

ULTUGAN. His relatives on his mother's side did an honest day's work and went to bed with a clear conscience. The ones who rushed around from morning till night getting nothing done came from your side of the family.

ISPANALI. Auntie, when will you stop listening in on every word we say? How long have you been here for? And where is our uncle Abdashim?

ULTUGAN. He's on the list, so he can't get away.

AUGANBEK. What list?

ULTUGAN. Your uncle wants to become an akim. He has put himself up for the elections.

ISPANALI. The elections? He wants to be an akim?

ULTUGAN. Eh, what's so surprising about that? Or do you think that Abdashim doesn't have the brains for it?

ISPANALI. How could we say something like that about our own relative?

But… well… he did finish school after the seventh grade...

ULTUGAN. You don't need an education to become a boss. In the old times the warriors didn't go to institutes and colleges like you, and they still ruled over people.

ISPANALI. That was a different time...

AUGANBEK. Eh, you... Some were station chiefs, some were workers' committees, when you were recommended for election you flatly refused, proudly saying 'we have our own work to do'...

ISPANALI. The boy laying in front of us also wants to become an akim. What is wrong with people? They don't even care whether they are able to govern people or not. They just don't care!

ULTUGAN. And that young mullah who came twice last week to read Bonaparte an incantation... The one who took three thousand tenge from us... He's also trying to become an akim.

AUGANBEK. Lord, forgive us! This is what people mean when they say "Be patient, Kazakh – you'll become an ataman [*Cossack leader*]!"

ULTUGAN. Cossack, not Kazakh, you idiot!

AUGANBEK. What's the difference? They sound almost the same! And by the way, Kazakhs were Cossacks once...

ULTUGAN. Your uncle has decided that he isn't going to get enough votes. He's asking me to call both of you to help him.

AUGANBEK. Well, honorary son-in-law, shall we

go?

ISPANALI. Let's resolve this problem first, then we'll see.

AUGANBEK. There's nothing to see – there's no point in going! Let them elect who they want. There isn't a single worthy man among them anyway.

ULTUGAN. I should be ashamed to call you a relative!

ISPANALI. Eh, Auntie – why do you get so cross at everything I say? Think about it – what does Abdashim need to be an akim for? Don't we already have enough problems? His son is lying here useless, not even able to talk. You'd be better off calling Abdashim back here. There is an urgent matter to attend to!

ULTUGAN. (*Gently stroking her son's hair*). Oh, my darling, I would do anything for you! I'm going to bring you a bowl of yummy soup.

Ultugan leaves quickly.

ISPANALI. Put those newspapers down! (*He rips them out of Bonaparte's hands*). What is it with this endless rest? Say something at least!

BONAPARTE. What can I say? You have all managed to say everything without me.

AUGANBEK. Listen, what on earth is a hot water

bottle doing here? (*He takes the hot water bottle from under the blanket*).

BONAPARTE. It's water...

AUGANBEK. If it's water then why are you hiding it under your blanket? (*He unscrews the top of the bottle and takes a sniff. He sniffs again, then tastes a drop of the liquid*). Eh, isn't this vodka? What is this, are you lying here and swigging vodka?

BONAPARTE. Well, the jigits brought it for me. They said it would help me to heal...

ISPANALI. Well I never! His breath smells of alcohol!

BONAPARTE. Um… well… All the same while I'm lying here I have nothing to do…

AUGANBEK. So now we know! And here was I wondering how he had turned into such an avid reader. It turns out he was trying to hide the smell... With 'medicine' like this you're not going to heal even in a year, have you got that?! (*He takes one swig of the vodka, then a bigger one*). You idiot! What moron do you have to be to keep vodka in a hot water bottle?

ISPANALI. Is it really vodka? Give it here (*He takes a small sip, then two big ones*). Well, if you're going to lie here drunk all day then you'll never get better! You're a drunk!

AUGANBEK. Your daddy is loitering around at

the club, and here you are lazing around here! (*He takes two more sips from the hot water bottle*).

ISPANALI. What a sage our aksakal Rat was – he obviously has a nose for these things. Remember what he said – where there is vodka, angels will never fly... (*He also takes the bottle and takes two sips*).

AUGANBEK. And who's bringing you the vodka?

BONAPARTE. Churchill and Roosevelt.

AUGANBEK. Ah yes – you are drinking in esteemed company! Tomorrow we're going to start changing all of your names. It has to be done. . What idiocy, that Kazakhs don't have enough names of their own...

BONAPARTE. What name are you going to choose?

ISPANALI. It's all our own fault... Auganbek, come here, let's sing together!

At that moment Bonaparte's little brother Chapai enters.

CHAPAI. Uncle Auganbek! Kashpirovsky's show is going to be on the television in an hour. Our whole village is going to watch it. They have even postponed the meeting at the club until tomorrow.

ISPANALI. Where is your father, if he isn't collecting the keys to the akim's office?

CHAPAI. They are also coming here. They told me to run here so you would have time to get ready.

AUGANBEK. Fine, we'll get ready. 'I have seen everything now' a woman once said, as she got ready to get married for the sixth time.

ISPANALI. By the way, you need to bring the television here and switch it on.

CHAPAI. There is no plug here. We need to go into the big house.

ISPANALI. Get up then, Sir Bonaparte. We are going to marvel at a hypnotist called Kashpirovsky. Perhaps he will free us from our own little ailments. Auganbek, help Sir Bonaparte to walk.

As music plays, Kashpirovsky opens his show.

KASHPIROVSKY. I'm not going to give names to your sicknesses. The magical power held inside my words will search for and find everything that is making you ill. A person's organism is made up of a special energy that we ourselves don't understand. I will awaken the source of this energy. The awoken energy will find any form of sickness and fight it by itself. During this show, try not to think about anything – you can even forget about your pains. You can think about me anything you like. I don't pay attention to such things. This is because I wish you only good things. And now you are falling into a pleasant dream and starting to fall asleep...

Either Kashpirovsky's soothing voice made them sleepy, or the alcohol had gone to their heads, but Auganbek and Ispanali's heads begin to drop, as they struggle to stay awake.

I'm giving an order. One, two, three, four...

AUGANBEK. (*With difficulty lifting his head*). Well? Is it working?

BONAPARTE. I don't know...

ISPANALI. As usual, then – you don't know. If you don't know then do I have to know?

AUGANBEK. Just relax and lie down!

ISPANALI. Don't be shy. We are all men here. Let Kashpirovsky see... Get it out and lie down!

KASHPIROVSKY. The healing of any illness depends on faith. If you genuinely believe, then my blessed words can work wonders from a thousand kilometres away. They hold the power of faith, the power of conviction. I believe you. I love you. I don't sleep at night, thinking about your health. Yes, I can feel that you are relaxed now. Close your eyes. Sleep soundly... Dream on, float free in the blue skies of your imagination... And now I will begin to wake you up. I'll count to ten: one, two, three, four…

AUGANBEK. Well, Bonaparte, do you feel any changes?

Bonaparte is silent.

Eh, he's already snoring! Let's take him back to his bed.

ISPANALI. Good grief, his father is snoring too! Abdashim, the show's over, you can get up.

ABDASHIM. (*In his sleep*). For the party "Tau-ekel"! Only forward!

ISPANALI. (*Laughing loudly*) Oh, stupid uncle of mine, what does politics need with you? They are both better off in bed.

Ultugan enters.

ULTUGAN. So, is there any hope he'll get better?

AUGANBEK. There is, Auntie, there is. Our little darling is fast asleep. God must have decided to lend a hand. While we carry these two, put them to bed and come back, then put out the dastarkhan. It's time it saw a feast!

ULTUGAN. Have you ever seen our dastarkhan

empty? Everything is already prepared, over there in the part of the house where the women sit!

ISPANALI. Well done, Auntie! You must come from a worthy family after all!

Both leave, supporting one another.

ABDASHIM. (*Still sleep-talking*). Long live the party "Praise to God"!

AUGANBEK. Long live it indeed!

***

A large stage. This could be Abdashim's house, but we don't have to explain where events are taking place. People are talking worriedly about something.

VOICES. – People, calm down!

–Tasbolat has returned from Austria.

– He will tell us all what the future holds for us.

– Oh my, we have been waiting for this for years. Does this village have a future?

– Here he is, let's welcome him. Here is the Tasbolat who has met and received an audience with the clairvoyant Globa!

– Wonderful!

– Tasbolat, welcome home! So tell us, what will our future be like?

TASBOLAT. The future will be good. The economy will pick up, incomes will grow, and life will be happier.

VOICES. – Your wishes will come true!

– This is music to our ears!

– What do we have to do? What did Globa say?

TASBOLAT. He said that we need to work.

VOICES. – He said what?

– What did you say?

– Say it again!

TASBOLAT. He said that we need to work.

VOICES. – Idiot!

– Cretin!

– We collected all that money to send you all that way... and that's all you found out?

– We don't need Globa to tell us we need to work!

– He should give us our money back!

– Just listen to this! Idiot! Cretin! Get him out of here!

– We should take him into the desert and leave him there!

The angry crowd lunges at Tasbolat. Tasbolat runs into the steppe. Everyone runs after him. Only Auganbek, Ispanali, Abdashim and Ultugan remain.

ABDASHIM. This is the end of the world! It's as if everyone has lost their mind!

AUGANBEK. It's not the end of the world. Everything is as it used to be. This is all our own fault.

ISPANALI. It isn't about whether Tasbolat went to see Globa or not. But there is something in what he said.

ULTUGAN. To hell with your meeting, and your

Globa. Is my boy getting enough rest?

Just then someone resembling a bear walks in. Everyone goes silent and freezes in fright.

AUGANBEK. Ah, it's… the village doctor, Rollan. Good evening!

ISPANALI. What are you doing here so late?

ULTUGAN. Come in, young man, come in...

ROLLAN. Which one of you called me a veterinarian?

In a crescendo:

– Why would we say something like that?! Heaven help us!

– May we all fall down with bird flu!

ROLLAN. Everyone should mind his own business. Don't you all go around spreading rumours, or I'll take this needle and put you all to sleep, have you got that?

ALL IN UNISON: – Of course! Got it!

– We understand!

ROLLAN. When they did the circumcision, some microbes got in. Even a third-rate vet would understand that. Your Bonaparte will get better. I've been coming here three days in a row, at night, to clean his wounds with medical spirit. Bonaparte! Come here and show yourself to your family and friends!

Bonaparte enters, wearing a white gown.
Everyone embraces him.

ULTUGAN. Is this real or am I dreaming? Oh my, doctor, my good young man, come and sit with us, have something to eat, I made this all myself.

ROLLAN. I don't have time now. I will come another time.

ABDASHIM. If you want you can come with us to bring the bride home..

ROLLAN. I have some bad news for you. Your son's future father-in-law has found out about your little misfortune, and out of shame has made a run for it in the direction of Syr-Darya!

VOICES. – Made a run for it? How?

– Our shame has caught up with us after all! This is the end of us!

– How are we going to look people in the eye?!

– Never mind that, how are we going to get our dowry back? We've already paid for half of it…

ROLLAN. It appears the girl was a strong one. She couldn't stand the shame, she ran away and tried to throw herself in the river with a rock around her neck. But two people caught up with her on horses and dragged her home. It sounds like she is still locked up in the house..

ULTUGAN. Well what do you expect, the poor girl has been through the same torture as our son. At least God stopped the disaster from happening!

AUGANBEK. You could say that both of them share the same fate. Love between people so young burns hotter than any fire...

ABDASHIM. But tell us, what must we do now?

ROLLAN. Show your slavish obedience, go and fall at their feet. Maybe they will forgive you..

ABDASHIM. And we won't have to do anything else?

ROLLAN. No, just be healthy!

The two say farewell to each other.
Then everyone surrounds Bonaparte,
looking him up and down.

AUGANBEK. Come on, show us how you can walk...

Bonaparte takes a couple of steps.

ISPANALI. Now jump!

Bonaparte climbs onto a chair and jumps off.

AUGANBEK. Not bad, Bonaparte! It wasn't for nothing that you spent the best part of a month laying in bed. (*To Ispanali*) And are you still sure that you're not going to play the replacement groom again?

ISPANALI. No chance! God will spare me…

AUGANBEK. Let's take our horses for a ride around the village tomorrow, what do you say, Bonaparte?

BONAPARTE. As you wish…

ABDASHIM. And what about the meeting tomorrow?

ISPANALI. Tomorrow you, aksakal Rat and I are going to hunt down that girl's father, fall at his feet and beg him to forgive us. You can forget about any meeting!

ULTUGAN. I'll go and pack you a bag.

Once again Bektur suddenly appears, and gives a speech to no-one in particular.

BEKTUR. The Baltimore City Court in the United States ordered the imprisonment for life of a Kazakh girl, Galiya Asanova, on false accusations of involvement in a murder. The Kazakh side did not even try to influence the course of the judicial investigation. Public organisations and representatives of the intelligentsia also silently ignored this decision. Wake up, Kazakh! Wake up, Kazakh!

He leaves.

ISPANALI. That man only ever appears when we are in the middle of a drama.

ULTUGAN. I told you that a brick fell on his head.

AUGANBEK. So let him go back to where it happened. What is he bothering us for? And what does he mean with all this "Wake up, Kazakh"?

Does he think we're sleeping?

ABDASHIM. I think he's just a bit simple. Maybe he is really the holy Kydyr-ata, who walks across the world's lands and oceans...

AUGANBEK. What holy man is going to appear at a time like this? They have probably long since disappeared from the face of the earth.

ABDASHIM. Still, it's worth thinking about...

ISPANALI. It's worth thinking about something else. Are we going to look for this girl's father tomorrow or not?

ABDASHIM. We've already agreed about that.

AUGANBEK. So, Bonaparte, son of Abdashim!

Are you ready to take yourself a bride?

BONAPARTE. That girl from before?

AUGANBEK. What are you talking about, that girl from before? Do you really not care which one it is?

BONAPARTE. Of course I care!

AUGANBEK. Then why are you talking nonsense like that? Let's prepare for tomorrow's journey!

***

The same cheerful music plays as it did at the beginning. Bonaparte's younger brother Chapai runs around the stage.

CHAPAI. Hooray! It's decided! Uncle Bonaparte is bringing his bride home tomorrow! Everyone is invited to the wedding! Come one, come all! Come and share our joy with us! There will be singing and dancing! Everybody come to the wedding!

END

REVIEW

Weddings have the capacity to bring great joy or invoke human fragility. With Bonaparte's Wedding Dulat Issabekov sets the bar high for dark comedy, with Kazakh traditions being challenged and a family in turmoil over a long-kept secret. Unfortunately secret's have a habit of being discovered..

A sense of foreboding is felt at the outset of the play with the congregating villagers lamenting "Now we've got the stench of this scandal on us, do we at least have the right to have our say about it?" This is in contrast with the innocent youthful exclamations preceding it of a young boy telling the village a Wedding shall be taking place very soon of his brother Bonaparte.

Unconventional and unrepenting seems to be one of the many surprises of Bonaparte's Wedding in the form of Bonaparte's parents Father Abdashim and Mother Ultugan, who very much echo their liberal son Bonaparte with their attitudes. With a carefree and measured approach to the potentially disastrous situation they are faced with about their soon to be married son, it is fascinating the quarrelling that takes place by judgemental Uncle's Auganbek and Ispanali as a result. Their referring of Bonaparte as an "infidel" is a huge insult to a muslim man, but the Uncle's old-fashioned views are often a cause of great humour with it's shock value and directness.

The play is one that relies on epic speeches and seem to be spoken from every character's mouth apart from Bonaparte, with Ultugan reminding her Uncle Ispanali he once told her "We mustn't let our horizons be narrowed by nationalism" because of pure criticism of his French name alone. The humour throughout is only heightened by the fact everyone has an opinion on the play's protagonist and his Wedding except him.

Bonaparte's Wedding is an extremely witty and intelligent look at tradition and redemption, showing just how complicated life can become when metaphorically the old and modern customs encounter each other face to face.

Francesca Mepham,
Theater critic, writer (UK).

REVIEW

'Bonaparte's Wedding' has been described as 'caustic' but anyone who has spent time in rural central Asia will see the imagery that Dulat Issabekov paints through his magical comedy play. The characters are all too familiar in every yurt community and the political and social changes that have occured over the past thirty years are picked out thread by thread. The overall 'tapestry' is more made of 'felt' that woven and if you close your eyes you can visualise the scenes, interiors and even the clothing people wear.

A comedic yet serious issue has the potential to derail the arranged marriage and the resulting involvement of village elders and busybodies leads to witty and insightful dialogue from colourful characters that are just waiting for a comedy actor's portrayal. It has the feel of a British Sitcom and even Monty Python and I can't wait to see it performed on the stage!

Gareth Stamp
Chairman Eurasian Creative guild

REVIEW

"Before Perestroika we had atheism"...A fascinating, humorous snapshot of post-Soviet village Kazakh life. Skillfully combining absurdity, cultural norms, Isabekov sets out a leftfield platform to joke on oft felt issues of extreme sensitivity. And what with Bonaparte, Roosevelt, and even Ho Chi Min offering naming rights to the locals we are in for a giant dollop of the ridiculous posing as the norm. Clearly a writer at the top of his game, delighting in the foibles that a newly claimed freedom exposes!

Warren Wills
Australian Director, composer, pianist

www.ingramcontent.com/pod-product-compliance
Lightning Source LLC
Chambersburg PA
CBHW041752010726
47507CB00009B/366

* 9 7 8 1 9 1 3 3 5 6 6 3 7 *